ENGLISCH MIT OXFORD

333 'Horror' Mistakes

Gillian and Peter Allison

Cornelsen
& OXFORD

ENGLISCH MIT OXFORD · 333 'Horror' Mistakes
wurde verfaßt von Gillian und Peter Allison in Zusammenarbeit mit der Verlagsredaktion.

Verlagsredaktion: Christine House
Illustrationen: Steven Garner, Colchester
Umschlagsgestaltung: Volker Noth, Grafik-Design, Berlin
Design und technische Umsetzung: Lynn Whittemore, Berlin

1. Auflage

3.	4.	5.	Die ersten Ziffern bezeichnen
94	95	96	Zahl und Jahr des Druckes

Druck: Saladruck, Berlin
Vertrieb: Cornelsen Verlag, Berlin

ISBN 3-8109-3585-9

Über dieses Buch

Vor ungefähr einem Jahr fragte ich in einer meiner Klassen einen neuen Schüler – einen 30jährigen deutschen Geschäftsmann –, ob er am Abend zuvor die Sendung über Skisport im Fernsehen gesehen habe. Uwe antwortete flüssig:

> "Yes, I have looked this two times in the television in the last time."

Ich verstand ihn natürlich, und ebenso verstanden ihn alle anderen in der Gruppe. Aber es wäre mir lieber gewesen, er hätte nicht so flüssig geantwortet. Die richtige Antwort wäre:

> "Yes, I have seen that twice on television recently".

Für erfahrene Lehrer sind Schüler wie Uwe gewohnte Figuren: Sie verstehen schnell, antworten, ohne lange nach den richtigen Wörtern zu suchen und können an den meisten Unterhaltungen teilnehmen.

Und das ist ihr größtes Problem.

Oft sind es intelligente, interessante Leute, die so begeistert diskutieren, daß es ihnen schwerfällt, lange genug abzuwarten, um sich die Korrekturen des Lehrers anzuhören.

Unterhalten sie sich dann jahrelang auf Englisch beispielsweise mit schwedischen oder französischen Geschäftspartnern, die nicht gewillt oder unfähig sind, sie auf ihre Fehler hinzuweisen, dann verfestigen sich ihre Sprachprobleme noch.

Es war schon immer unsere Erfahrung, daß die schweren grammatikalischen Fehler einfacher zu eliminieren sind als die leichteren – diejenigen, die für uns zu 'Horror' mistakes geworden sind.

Dieses Buch ist entstanden, um den Uwes dieser Welt zu helfen. Es kann zum Selbststudium zu Hause oder für den Unterricht in der Klasse benutzt werden.

Einführung

Während der letzten paar Jahre haben wir jeden Fehler, den unsere Schüler machten, sorgfältig aufgeschrieben. Viele waren natürlich sogenannte Zeitfehler, aber langsam begann sich eine andere Kategorie aus unseren Notizbüchern herauszukristallisieren – 333 sich ständig wiederholende Fehler und „unenglische" Ausdrücke, kurz 'Horror' mistakes.

Viele dieser „unenglischen" Ausdrücke sind strenggenommen keine grammatikalischen Fehler. Es ist beispielsweise nicht falsch zu sagen: "I have too little time" oder "He has much money". Aber beides klingt sehr fremd, und Engländer würden es normalerweise so formulieren: "I haven't got enough time" und "He's got a lot of money".

Diese 333 'Horrors' wurden in 59 Listen mit je 30 Sätzen verteilt, von denen jeder nur einen – und **nur** einen – typischen Fehler enthält. Den 30 „falschen" Sätzen auf der linken Seite stehen jeweils die „korrekten" Sätze auf der rechten Seite gegenüber. Diese 'Oxford English'-Sätze stellen lediglich eine Version des Standardenglisch dar.

Die in Klammern stehenden zahlen hinter den 'Oxford English'-Sätzen verweisen auf die entsprechenden Erklärungen im Grammatikteil am Ende des Buches.

Die Lernenden sollten zunächst die „korrekte" Liste auf der rechten Seite abdecken und versuchen, die Sätze auf der linken Seite zu korrigieren. Jeder Fehler erscheint in den englischen Satzlisten vier- oder fünfmal. Die deutsch-englischen Übersetzungsübungen, die in regelmäßigen Abständen eingestreut sind, dienen dazu, das Gelernte im aktiven Wortschatz zu verfestigen. Das ganze Buch ist angelegt als riesige Schleife, in der sich kleinere Schleifen aus je fünf Seiten befinden. Ist das Ende des Buches erreicht, kann man bei Bedarf einfach zur ersten Seite zurückkehren und erneut anfangen!

Die „echten" Fehler unserer Schüler wurden leicht verändert, um sie einfacher verständlich zu machen, so daß auch jemand mit geringen Englischkenntnissen aus diesem Buch Nutzen ziehen kann.

Untersuchungen haben gezeigt, daß sogar jene, die wirkliche Probleme mit der Grammatik haben, unsere „Fehlerschleife“ als einfache, schnelle und angenehme Art und Weise ansehen, modernes und korrektes Englisch zu erlernen. (Wenn Ihr Englisch jetzt schon gut ist, wird es bald perfekt sein!)

Der Schwerpunkt in diesem Buch· liegt auf dem alltäglich gesprochenen Englisch im Gegensatz zur formalen Schriftsprache.

Bei dieser Gelegenheit möchten wir alle Englischlernenden (und speziell unsere eigenen Schüler) an das Geheimnis der Beherrschung einer Sprache erinnern:

Wiederholung, Wiederholung, Wiederholung!

Wir wünschen VIEL ERFOLG!

Die Autoren

6 'HORROR' MISTAKES

1 The garage is a great building.
2 How do you call that in English?
3 That's the car from the boss.
4 When did you marry?
5 I'm not working in the moment.
6 Your perfume smells well.
7 He's got much wine in the cellar.
8 I don't understand this things.
9 With what did you open the door?
10 Hot is the opposite from cold.
11 He play tennis every week.
12 The most people live in cities.
13 When have you birthday?
14 He's so an important man.
15 Please may I have the book?
16 That what you said isn't true.
17 I was reading in the paper when the bus arrived.
18 I would like that he does it.
19 We saw the game in television last week.
20 "Rome's the capital of Italy." – "I know it."
21 It gives four theatres in the town.
22 If he would understand, it would be easier.
23 We drove to Bonn with the car yesterday.
24 Do you mean the weather will be better tomorrow?
25 The door is of metal.
26 I phoned with John yesterday.
27 The TV tower is a tall house.
28 That's something what we don't need.
29 A factory is a place where men work in.
30 He has been working by Thyssen for years.

1 The garage is a **big** building. (20)
2 **What** do you call that in English? (10)
3 That's the **boss's** car. (3)
4 When did you **get married**? (21)
5 I'm not working **at** the moment. (11)
6 Your perfume smells **good**. (58)
7 He's got **a lot of** wine in the cellar. (22)
8 I don't understand **these** things. (12)
9 **What** did you open the door **with**? (28)
10 Hot is the opposite **of** cold. (18)
11 He **plays** tennis every week. (8)
12 **Most** people live in cities. (29)
13 When **is your** birthday? (19)
14 He's **such** an important man. (14)
15 May I have the book, **please**? (4)
16 **What** you said isn't true. (25)
17 I was **reading** the paper when the bus arrived. (1)
18 I would like **him to do** it. (23)
19 We saw the game **on** television last week. (9)
20 "Rome's the capital of Italy." – "**I know**." (2)
21 **There are** four theatres in the town. (24)
22 If he **understood**, it would be easier. (15)
23 We **drove** to Bonn yesterday. (5)
24 Do you **think** the weather will be better tomorrow? (26)
25 The door is **made** of metal. (16)
26 I **phoned** John yesterday. (6)
27 The TV tower is a tall **building**. (27)
28 That's **something** we don't need. (17)
29 A factory is a place where men **work**. (7)
30 He has been working **for** Thyssen for years. (13)

1 Die Rosen riechen wunderbar.
2 Das ist das Haus der Kochs.
3 Ich las gerade in einem Buch, als sie kam.
4 „Schmidt ist sehr reich." – „Ich weiß es."
5 Darf ich bitte ein anderes Glas haben?
6 Er ist gestern mit dem Wagen nach Paderborn gefahren.
7 Ich habe gestern mit Monika telefoniert.
8 Eine Tasse ist ein Gegenstand, woraus man trinkt.
9 Sie liest jeden Tag die Zeitung.
10 Ich habe es gestern im Radio gehört.
11 Wie heißt das auf deutsch?
12 Er ist im Moment nicht hier.
13 Diese Sachen sind für dich.
14 Er arbeitet bei IKEA.
15 Das ist so eine schöne Katze.
16 Wenn er das sehen würde, würde er es verstehen.
17 Der Tisch ist aus Holz.
18 Das ist etwas, was ich nie gehört habe.
19 Was ist das Gegenteil von „trocken"?
20 Ich habe morgen Geburtstag.
21 Sie arbeitet in einem großen Gebäude.
22 Sie hat letztes Jahr geheiratet.
23 Er hat viel Geld.
24 Ich will, daß sie morgen früher kommt.
25 Es gibt zwei Hotels im Dorf.
26 Das, was er sagte, habe ich nicht verstanden.
27 Ich glaube, morgen wird die Sonne scheinen.
28 In diesem Haus arbeiten nur Fachleute.
29 Mit wem haben Sie gesprochen?
30 Die meisten Katzen schlafen viel.

1 The roses smell wonderful. (58)
2 That's the Kochs' house. (3)
3 I was reading a book when she came. (1)
4 "Schmidt is very rich." – "I know." (2)
5 May I have a different glass, please? (4)
6 He drove to Paderborn yesterday. (5)
7 I phoned Monika yesterday. (6)
8 A cup is an object you drink from. (7)
9 She reads the newspaper every day. (8)
10 I heard it on the radio yesterday. (9)
11 What do you call that in German? (10)
12 He's not here at the moment. (11)
13 These things are for you. (12)
14 He works for IKEA. (13)
15 That's such a beautiful cat. (14)
16 If he saw that, he would understand it. (15)
17 The table is made of wood. (16)
18 That's something I've never heard. (17)
19 What's the opposite of "dry"? (18)
20 It's my birthday tomorrow. (19)
21 She works in a big building. (20)
22 She got married last year. (21)
23 He's got a lot of money. (22)
24 I want her to come earlier tomorrow. (23)
25 There are two hotels in the village. (24)
26 I didn't understand what he said. (25)
27 I think the sun will shine tomorrow. (26)
28 Only specialists work in this building. (27)
29 Who did you speak to? (28)
30 Most cats sleep a lot. (29)

10 'HORROR' MISTAKES

1 In which room do you work?
2 A lorry is a great vehicle.
3 I saw the same machine by Karstadt last week.
4 I think the Smiths are very nice peoples.
5 The most dogs have a good life.
6 Where did they marry?
7 She's so an attractive lady.
8 The garden looks well.
9 We were invited to a party from our neighbours.
10 We've got much free time this week.
11 If she would see it, she would understand it.
12 She go to the cinema every Friday.
13 "Had you to work yesterday?" – "Yes, I had." / "No, I hadn't."
14 She wants that we do the work at once.
15 The desk is of wood.
16 Squash isn't often in TV.
17 He has to bring the children to school before he goes to work.
18 It gives a lot of pubs in the city centre.
19 Those are the books what we should buy.
20 How do they call "beer" in French?
21 We see us this evening!
22 That what I told you yesterday is wrong.
23 Clean is the opposite from dirty.
24 She's writing a letter in the moment.
25 1940? I wasn't even born at this time.
26 Do you mean you could do his job?
27 I have birthday in May.
28 This books are for you.
29 I spoke to her on a party last week.
30 The museum is a large house.

1 **Which** room do you work **in**? (28)
2 A lorry is a **big** vehicle. (20)
3 I saw the same machine **at** Karstadt last week. (13)
4 I think the Smiths are very nice **people**. (182)
5 **Most** dogs have a good life. (29)
6 Where did they **get married**? (21)
7 She's **such** an attractive lady. (14)
8 The garden looks **good**. (58)
9 We were invited to a party **by** our neighbours. (30)
10 We've got **a lot of** free time this week. (22)
11 If she **saw** it, she would understand it. (15)
12 She **goes** to the cinema every Friday. (8)
13 "**Did** you **have to** work yesterday?" – "Yes, I **did**." / "No, I **didn't**." (31)
14 She wants **us to do** the work at once. (23)
15 The desk is **made** of wood. (16)
16 Squash isn't often **on** TV. (9)
17 He has to **take** the children to school before he goes to work. (34)
18 **There are** a lot of pubs in the city centre. (24)
19 Those are the **books** we should buy. (17)
20 **What** do they call "beer" in French? (10)
21 **See you** this evening! (35)
22 **What** I told you yesterday is wrong. (25)
23 Clean is the opposite **of** dirty. (18)
24 She's writing a letter **at** the moment. (11)
25 1940? I wasn't even born at **that** time. (32)
26 Do you **think** you could do his job? (26)
27 **My** birthday **is** in May. (19)
28 **These** books are for you. (12)
29 I spoke to her **at** a party last week. (33)
30 The museum is a large **building**. (27)

12 'HORROR' MISTAKES

1. To whom are you writing?
2. My wife has much patience.
3. That what he has written is good.
4. When has your mother birthday?
5. How many peoples were at the party?
6. 1977? I was still living in Cologne at this time.
7. Do you ever have a chance to train your English?
8. He means he can do the job.

9. The factory is a great, dirty building.
10. The meat tastes well.
11. His job is the same like mine.
12. I was on a party last night.
13. We married in May.
14. It was a two-days trip to Milan.
15. I brought the car to the garage yesterday.

16. We stood in Dover for one day before going to London.
17. "Have you to go to Munich again?" – "Yes, I have." / "No, I haven't."
18. The chair is of steel.
19. We see us tomorrow!
20. Did you inform yourself about the new timetable?
21. The most people go on holiday in the summer.
22. I expect that she types the report today.
23. A TV is something what everybody needs.

24. He speaks French also.
25. If you get up tomorrow, go and buy some bread.
26. The cake was made from his wife.
27. It gave a lot of trouble at the demonstration.
28. What's the opposite from rich?
29. Over a hundred people work in the house.
30. If they would hear the report, they would know everything.

1. **Who** are you writing **to**? (28)
2. My wife has **a lot of** patience. (22)
3. **What** he has written is good. (25)
4. When **is** your mother**'s** birthday? (19)
5. How many **people** were at the party? (182)
6. 1977? I was still living in Cologne at **that** time. (32)
7. Do you ever have a chance to **practise** your English? (38)
8. He **thinks** he can do the job. (26)
9. The factory is a **big**, dirty building. (20)
10. The meat tastes **good**. (58)
11. His job is the same **as** mine. (39)
12. I was **at** a party last night. (33)
13. We **got married** in May. (21)
14. It was a two-**day** trip to Milan. (40)
15. I **took** the car to the garage yesterday. (34)
16. We **stayed** in Dover for one day before going to London. (37)
17. "**Do** you **have to** go to Munich again?" – "Yes, I **do**." / "No, I **don't**." (31)
18. The chair is **made** of steel. (16)
19. **See you** tomorrow! (35)
20. Did you **find out** about the new timetable? (41)
21. **Most** people go on holiday in the summer. (29)
22. I expect **her to type** the report today. (23)
23. A TV is **something** everybody needs. (17)
24. He **also** speaks French. (42)
25. **When** you get up tomorrow, go and buy some bread. (36)
26. The cake was made **by** his wife. (30)
27. **There was** a lot of trouble at the demonstration. (24)
28. What's the opposite **of** rich? (18)
29. Over a hundred people work in the **building**. (27)
30. If they **heard** the report, they would know everything. (15)

1 Most time we stay at home at Christmas.
2 Last year I had a four-weeks holiday.
3 We see us later!
4 The picture was painted from Leonardo.
5 That what I saw was terrible.
6 I've never seen so many peoples.
7 I could drive with eighteen.
8 I informed myself about the holidays before I took the job.
9 When it rains tomorrow, we'll stay at home.
10 "Have you to come here tomorrow?" – "Yes, I have." / "No, I haven't."
11 I mean the boss is a hard man.
12 His new LP sounds wonderfully.
13 The bank robber went to the prison for five years.
14 You can buy them here and you can buy them in England also.
15 We stood in Florence for three days last summer.
16 The World Cup in Germany? – We were in England at this time.
17 The factory is a big house.
18 They have got much work at the moment.
19 Adenauer is died.
20 It's not worth to die for that.
21 I used to train the piano every day.
22 Were you on the party last Friday?
23 At which desk do you work?
24 The boss wants that you work overtime.
25 Where do you cut the bread with?
26 Where did you go at Eastern?
27 My car is the same like John's.
28 I had to bring my son to school yesterday.
29 The most houses have got central heating.
30 It gives two good teams in the city.

1 **Normally** we stay at home at Christmas. (46)
2 Last year I had a four-**week** holiday. (40)
3 **See you** later! (35)
4 The picture was painted **by** Leonardo. (30)
5 **What** I saw was terrible. (25)
6 I've never seen so many **people**. (182)
7 I could drive **at** eighteen. (47)
8 I **found out** about the holidays before I took the job. (41)
9 **If** it rains tomorrow, we'll stay at home. (36)
10 "**Do** you **have to** come here tomorrow?" – "Yes, I **do**." / "No, I **don't**." (31)
11 I **think** the boss is a hard man. (26)
12 His new LP sounds **wonderful**. (58)
13 The bank robber went **to prison** for five years. (48)
14 You can buy them here and you can **also** buy them in England. (42)
15 We **stayed** in Florence for three days last summer. (37)
16 The World Cup in Germany? – We were in England at **that** time. (32)
17 The factory is a big **building.** (27)
18 They have got **a lot of** work at the moment. (22)
19 Adenauer is **dead**. (49)
20 It's not worth **dying** for that. (43)
21 I used to **practise** the piano every day. (38)
22 Were you **at** the party last Friday? (33)
23 **Which** desk do you work **at**? (28)
24 The boss wants **you to work** overtime. (23)
25 **What** do you cut the bread with? (51)
26 Where did you go at **Easter**? (45)
27 My car is the same **as** John's. (39)
28 I had to **take** my son to school yesterday. (34)
29 **Most** houses have got central heating. (29)
30 **There are** two good teams in the city. (24)

16 'HORROR' MISTAKES

1 I have hunger. May I have a sandwich, please?
2 "I'm twenty today." – "Congratulations!"
3 Did you inform yourself about other cars before buying a Jaguar?
4 We went for a two-hours walk on Sunday.
5 Half past three yesterday? I was still in the office at this time.
6 What does it say on the backside of the book?
7 If I am sixty-five, I'll retire.
8 My feets are like blocks of ice.
9 Where do you write with?
10 Most time they go skiing in the winter.
11 What did you do at Eastern?
12 Mao is died many years ago.
13 I have any problems.
14 He stood in Italy for more than two years.
15 We met on a party two weeks ago.
16 The roses smell beautifully.
17 I have to visit Rome twice in the next time.
18 Have you visited Spain in the last time?
19 She could cook well with fourteen.
20 I like tennis, and I like squash also.
21 I never have a chance to train my French.
22 I brought my wife to the station before driving to the office.
23 The work was done from an expert.
24 We had no money for a holiday and for this reason we stayed at home.
25 You can see there exotic animals.
26 The patient spent two weeks in the hospital.
27 It's not worth to learn Arabic.
28 Her dress is the same like my sister's.
29 We see us at the party!
30 "Has he to drive a lot?" – "Yes, he has." / "No, he hasn't."

1 I **am hungry**. May I have a sandwich, please? (53)

2 "I'm twenty today." – "**Happy Birthday**!" (60)

3 Did you **find out** about other cars before buying a Jaguar? (41)

4 We went for a two-**hour** walk on Sunday. (40)

5 Half past three yesterday? I was still in the office at **that** time. (32)

6 What does it say on the **back** of the book? (52)

7 **When** I am sixty-five, I'll retire. (36)

8 My **feet** are like blocks of ice. (182)

9 **What** do you write with? (51)

10 **Normally** they go skiing in the winter. (46)

11 What did you do at **Easter**? (45)

12 Mao **died** many years ago. (49)

13 I have **some** problems. (54)

14 He **stayed** in Italy for more than two years. (37)

15 We met **at** a party two weeks ago. (33)

16 The roses smell **beautiful**. (58)

17 I have to visit Rome twice in the **near future**. (57)

18 Have you visited Spain **recently**? (56)

19 She could cook well **at** fourteen. (47)

20 I like tennis, and I **also** like squash. (42)

21 I never have a chance to **practise** my French. (38)

22 I **took** my wife to the station before driving to the office. (34)

23 The work was done **by** an expert. (30)

24 We had no money for a holiday and **that's why** we stayed at home. (59)

25 You can see exotic animals **there**. (55)

26 The patient spent two weeks **in hospital**. (48)

27 It's not worth **learning** Arabic. (43)

28 Her dress is the same **as** my sister's. (39)

29 **See you** at the party! (35)

30 "**Does** he **have to** drive a lot?" – "Yes, he **does**." / "No, he **doesn't**." (31)

1 Dieser Stoff fühlt sich gut an.
2 Pfui! Deine Füße sind schmutzig!
3 Das Buch wurde von einer Frau geschrieben.
4 „Müssen Sie gehen?" – „Ja, ich muß." / „Nein, ich muß nicht."
5 1980? – Ich war zu dieser Zeit in Hamburg.
6 Ich habe sie auf einer Party kennengelernt.
7 Sie brachten den Mann ins Krankenhaus.
8 Wir sehen uns nächste Woche!
9 Wenn mein Mann nach Hause kommt, werden wir essen.
10 Wir sind übers Wochenende in Köln geblieben.
11 Ich sollte mein Englisch viel mehr trainieren.
12 Das Bild dort drüben ist das gleiche wie dieses hier.
13 Unser zweiwöchiger Urlaub war sehr schön.
14 Ich werde mich informieren, wer das gemacht hat.
15 Das sind auch Nachbarn von uns.
16 Es lohnt sich nicht, mit ihm darüber zu reden.
17 Was habt ihr zu Ostern gemacht?
18 Meistens bleiben wir zu Hause.
19 Sie konnte mit neun schon schwimmen.
20 Der Mörder kam ins Gefängnis.
21 Seine Frau ist letztes Jahr gestorben.
22 Womit schreiben Sie?
23 Was steht auf der Rückseite des Buches?
24 Ich habe Hunger.
25 Ich sah draußen jemanden.
26 Man findet dort nur teure Sachen.
27 Ich habe ihn in letzter Zeit nicht gesehen.
28 In nächster Zeit gibt es keine Feste mehr.
29 Er war krank, und aus diesem Grund blieb er zu Hause.
30 „Ich bin heute zweiundzwanzig geworden!" – „Herzlichen Glückwunsch!"

1 This cloth feels good. (58)
2 Ugh! Your feet are dirty! (182)
3 The book was written by a woman. (30)
4 "Do you have to go?" – "Yes, I do." / "No, I don't." (31)
5 1980? – I was in Hamburg at that time. (32)
6 I met her at a party. (33)
7 They took the man to hospital. (34)
8 See you next week! (35)
9 When my husband gets home, we'll eat. (36)
10 We stayed in Cologne over the weekend. (37)
11 I should practise my English a lot more. (38)
12 The picture over there is the same as this one here. (39)
13 Our two-week holiday was very nice. (40)
14 I'll find out who did that. (41)
15 They are also neighbours of ours. (42)
16 It's not worth talking to him about it. (43)
17 What did you do at Easter? (45)
18 Normally we stay at home. (46)
19 She could swim at nine. (47)
20 The murderer went to prison. (48)
21 His wife died last year. (49)
22 What do you write with? (51)
23 What does it say on the back of the book? (52)
24 I am hungry. (53)
25 I saw somebody outside. (54)
26 You only find expensive things there. (55)
27 I haven't seen him lately. (56)
28 There'll be no more parties in the near future. (57)
29 He was ill, and so he stayed at home. (59)
30 "I'm twenty-two today!" – "Happy birthday!" (60)

1 He came here one time last week.
2 He lost his job and for this reason he's depressed.
3 He was able to talk with two years.

4 Their house is the same like ours.
5 He has seen anything unusual.
6 We went away at Eastern.
7 You should train your English more.
8 Childrens make a lot of noise.
9 This is a photo from my cat.
10 They are friends of ours also.
11 He has a sport car.
12 Where do we eat with?
13 Most times she drinks coffee.
14 It's not worth to buy a bigger car.
15 That dessert tasted wonderfully.
16 The both colleagues were angry.
17 He is a colleague of me.
18 Have you seen John in the last time?
19 I have thirst. May I have a drink, please?
20 I read about Franco's dead in the newspaper.
21 It's only a five-minutes walk to the station.
22 When it's a hard winter, I'll fly to Spain.
23 We have got too few holidays.
24 You can find there interesting books.
25 "I'm forty today." – "Congratulations!"
26 In the next time there'll be a new model on the market.
27 We must inform ourselves about the situation.
28 The garden is at the backside of the house.
29 They go to the church on Sundays.
30 She stood in London for two days.

1. He came here **once** last week. (63)
2. He lost his job and **that's why** he's depressed. (59)
3. He was able to talk **at two**. (47)
4. Their house is the same **as** ours. (39)
5. He has seen **something** unusual. (54)
6. We went away at **Easter**. (45)
7. You should **practise** your English more. (38)
8. **Children** make a lot of noise. (182)
9. This is a photo **of** my cat. (61)
10. They are **also** friends of ours. (42)
11. He has a **sports** car. (65)
12. **What** do we eat with? (51)
13. **Normally** she drinks coffee. (46)
14. It's not worth **buying** a bigger car. (43)
15. That dessert tasted **wonderful**. (58)
16. **Both** colleagues were angry. (66)
17. He is a colleague of **mine**. (64)
18. Have you seen John **lately**? (56)
19. I **am thirsty**. May I have a drink, please? (53)
20. I read about Franco's **death** in the newspaper. (49)
21. It's only a five-**minute** walk to the station. (40)
22. **If** it's a hard winter, I'll fly to Spain. (36)
23. We have**n't** got **enough** holidays. (62)
24. You can find interesting books **there**. (55)
25. "I'm forty today." – "**Happy Birthday**!" (60)
26. In the **near future** there'll be a new model on the market. (57)
27. We must **find out** about the situation. (41)
28. The garden is at the **back** of the house. (52)
29. They go **to church** on Sundays. (48)
30. She **stayed** in London for two days. (37)

1 This is our sport club.
2 We catched two fish yesterday.
3 She went for a walk two times at the weekend.
4 She found a nice flat and for this reason she's happy.
5 You can buy there cheap cameras.
6 They were standing at the backside of the building.
7 The Eastern holiday is too short.
8 She goes to the night school twice a week.
9 Peoples can be very stupid.
10 It's a really pleasure to meet you.
11 My first woman was a great cook.
12 He's got too few friends here.
13 "I'm thirty-one today." – "Congratulations!"
14 There is anybody outside.
15 Churchill is died.
16 He has hunger. He wants something to eat.
17 Most times she watches television in the evening.
18 Those flowers look beautifully.
19 "What's the score?" – "One – three."
20 The winner became a wonderful prize.
21 Here's a photo from my house.
22 She's a neighbour of him.
23 We'll have to book our holidays in the next time.
24 Has he visited his mother in the last time?
25 Where do you put the plates on?
26 He was able to read with six years.
27 It's not worth to work overtime.
28 The both women were Italian.
29 Have you knowledges of French?
30 347 = three hundred forty-seven.

1 This is our **sports** club. (65)
2 We **caught** two fish yesterday. (72)
3 She went for a walk **twice** at the weekend. (63)
4 She found a nice flat and **that's why** she's happy. (59)
5 You can buy cheap cameras **there**. (55)
6 They were standing at the **back** of the building. (52)
7 The **Easter** holiday is too short. (45)
8 She goes **to night school** twice a week. (48)
9 **People** can be very stupid. (182)
10 It's a **real** pleasure to meet you. (71)
11 My first **wife** was a great cook. (67)
12 He has**n't** got **enough** friends here. (62)
13 "I'm thirty-one today." – "**Happy Birthday**!" (60)
14 There is **somebody** outside. (54)
15 Churchill is **dead**. (49)
16 He **is hungry**. He wants something to eat. (53)
17 **Normally** she watches television in the evening. (46)
18 Those flowers look **beautiful**. (58)
19 "What's the score?" – "**Three – one**." (73)
20 The winner **got** a wonderful prize. (68)
21 Here's a photo **of** my house. (61)
22 She's a neighbour of **his**. (64)
23 We'll have to book our holidays in the **near future**. (57)
24 Has he visited his mother **lately**? (56)
25 **What** do you put the plates on? (51)
26 He was able to read **at six**. (47)
27 It's not worth **working** overtime. (43)
28 **Both** women were Italian. (66)
29 **Do** you **know any French**? (69)
30 347 = three hundred **and** forty-seven. (70)

'HORROR' MISTAKES

1 We've been living here for one and a half year.
2 Did you see the play between Liverpool and Munich?
3 The murderer was catched in forty-eight hours.
4 How good are your knowledges of English?
5 Did I show you the picture from my dog?
6 Are you going to see Susan in the next time?
7 She has thirst. She wants something to drink.
8 How many womans were here yesterday?
9 He doesn't his work well.
10 "What's the score?" – "Two – three."
11 101 = one hundred one.
12 I first met my woman twenty years ago.
13 They're friends of us.
14 He hasn't got some money.
15 It's a really problem.
16 This material feels softly.

17 The both houses were very nice.
18 The little girl was angry to ride on a big horse.
19 "I'm fifty today." – "Congratulations!"
20 You can learn there Spanish.
21 I made the same mistake two times.
22 There's a fast street between Manchester and Liverpool.
23 There isn't place in my office for another desk.
24 How much money did the winner become?
25 He bought a small sport boat last week.
26 She's got too few hobbies.
27 Thirty degrees in the shadow was too hot for me.
28 I have a good job and for this reason I'm satisfied.
29 Have you been to the theatre in the last time?
30 There's nothing on the backside of the poster.

1 We've been living here for one and a half **years**. (81)
2 Did you see the **game** between Liverpool and Munich? (75)
3 The murderer was **caught** in forty-eight hours. (72)
4 How good **is your English**? (69)
5 Did I show you the picture **of** my dog? (61)
6 Are you going to see Susan in the **near future**? (57)
7 She **is thirsty**. She wants something to drink. (53)
8 How many **women** were here yesterday? (182)
9 He **doesn't do** his work well. (80)
10 "What's the score?" – "**Three – two**." (73)
11 101 = one hundred **and** one. (70)
12 I first met my **wife** twenty years ago. (67)
13 They're friends of **ours**. (64)
14 He hasn't got **any** money. (54)
15 It's a **real** problem. (71)
16 This material feels **soft**. (58)
17 **Both** houses were very nice. (66)
18 The little girl was **afraid** to ride on a big horse. (78)
19 "I'm fifty today." – "**Happy Birthday**!" (60)
20 You can learn Spanish **there**. (55)
21 I made the same mistake **twice**. (63)
22 There's a fast **road** between Manchester and Liverpool. (77)
23 There isn't **room** in my office for another desk. (74)
24 How much money did the winner **get**? (68)
25 He bought a small **sports** boat last week. (65)
26 She has**n't** got **enough** hobbies. (62)
27 Thirty degrees in the **shade** was too hot for me. (76)
28 I have a good job and **that's why** I'm satisfied. (59)
29 Have you been to the theatre **lately**? (56)
30 There's nothing on the **back** of the poster. (52)

1 He painted a picture from his mother.
2 It's a hobby of her.
3 Where did you meet your woman?
4 621 = six hundred twenty-one.
5 The street between Bingen and St Goar is very beautiful.
6 Look at the shade of my hand on the wall!
7 What do you in the evening?
8 What colour has your new pullover?
9 Tom was drunken at the party.
10 They come usually late.
11 There are eleven mens in a team.
12 The station is direct at the end of the street.
13 He always wears a sport jacket.
14 A doctor becomes more money than an electrician.
15 That could become a really problem.
16 Ice hockey is a very fast play.
17 Cologne is winning: nil – one.
18 I've been waiting for you for one and a half hour.
19 The both holidays were expensive.
20 What's with a coffee?
21 You've got too few interests.
22 This cloth feels well.
23 They went there one time last year.
24 How many persons were killed in the accident?
25 My Italian knowledges are not so good.
26 The prisoners were catched again the same day.
27 There isn't place in my cellar for a table-tennis table.
28 The boy was angry to go on the ghost-train alone.
29 When I come home from work, I always lay on the sofa for one hour.
30 I've never seen a fox in the nature.

1 He painted a picture **of** his mother. (61)
2 It's a hobby of **hers**. (64)
3 Where did you meet your **wife**? (67)
4 621 = six hundred **and** twenty-one. (70)
5 The **road** between Bingen and St Goar is very beautiful. (77)
6 Look at the **shadow** of my hand on the wall! (76)
7 What **do** you **do** in the evening? (80)
8 What colour **is** your new pullover? (83)
9 Tom was **drunk** at the party. (86)
10 They **usually** come late. (85)
11 There are eleven **men** in a team. (182)
12 The station is **right** at the end of the street. (89)
13 He always wears a **sports** jacket. (65)
14 A doctor **gets** more money than an electrician. (68)
15 That could become a **real** problem. (71)
16 Ice hockey is a very fast **game**. (75)
17 Cologne is winning: **one – nil**. (73)
18 I've been waiting for you for one and a half **hours**. (81)
19 **Both** holidays were expensive. (66)
20 **What about** a coffee? (87)
21 You have**n't** got **enough** interests. (62)
22 This cloth feels **good**. (58)
23 They went there **once** last year. (63)
24 How many **people** were killed in the accident? (84)
25 My **Italian is** not so good. (69)
26 The prisoners were **caught** again the same day. (72)
27 There isn't **room** in my cellar for a table-tennis table. (74)
28 The boy was **afraid** to go on the ghost-train alone. (78)
29 When I come home from work, I always **lie** on the sofa for one hour. (82)
30 I've never seen a fox in the **wild**. (88)

1 Die neuen Nachbarn sind sehr nette Leute.
2 Dein neues Parfüm riecht gut.
3 Das ist ein Bild von meinem Wohnzimmer.
4 Wir haben zu wenig Geld.
5 Ich habe sie diese Woche einmal gesehen.
6 Das ist John, ein Freund von mir.
7 Tom will sich einen Sportwagen kaufen.
8 Die beiden Männer waren Freunde.
9 Ich liebe meine Frau.
10 Der Sieger bekam das Geld.
11 Meine Spanischkenntnisse könnten besser sein.
12 201 = zweihunderteins.
13 Das könnte ein echtes Problem werden.
14 Der Mörder wurde zwei Stunden später gefangen.
15 Bayern führt eins zu null in Köln.
16 Im Büro ist kein Platz für einen Computer.
17 Schach ist ein gutes Spiel für Kinder.
18 Es waren dreißig Grad im Schatten.
19 Die Straße zwischen Kaarst und Osterath ist nicht sehr breit.
20 Das Kind hatte Angst, das Haus alleine zu betreten.
21 Sie macht ihre Arbeit nicht gut.
22 Das Spiel dauert anderthalb Stunden.
23 Leg dich hin und mach die Augen zu!
24 Welche Farbe hat die Wand?
25 Es waren fünfzig Personen im Raum.
26 Sie trinken immer Rotwein.
27 Er war gar nicht betrunken.
28 Wie wär's mit einer Tasse Tee?
29 Ich habe nur einmal einen Löwen in der Natur gesehen.
30 Mein Schreibtisch ist direkt neben dem Fenster.

1 The new neighbours are very nice people. (182)
2 Your new perfume smells good. (58)
3 This is a picture of my living-room. (61)
4 We haven't got enough money. (62)
5 I've seen her once this week. (63)
6 This is John, a friend of mine. (64)
7 Tom wants to buy a sports car. (65)
8 The two men were friends. (66)
9 I love my wife. (67)
10 The winner got the money. (68)
11 My Spanish could be better. (69)
12 201 = two hundred and one. (70)
13 That could become a real problem. (71)
14 The murderer was caught two hours later. (72)
15 Bayern is leading one – nil in Cologne. (73)
16 There's no room for a computer in the office. (74)
17 Chess is a good game for children. (75)
18 It was thirty degrees in the shade. (76)
19 The road between Kaarst and Osterath isn't very wide. (77)
20 The child was afraid to enter the house alone. (78)
21 She doesn't do her work well. (80)
22 The game lasts one and a half hours. (81)
23 Lie down and close your eyes! (82)
24 What colour is the wall? (83)
25 There were fifty people in the room. (84)
26 They always drink red wine. (85)
27 He wasn't drunk at all. (86)
28 What about a cup of tea? (87)
29 I've only once seen a lion in the wild. (88)
30 My desk is right next to the window. (89)

1 "Must you go so early?" – "No, I mustn't."
2 Is there place in your flat for fifty guests?
3 He looked drunken.
4 All people here are French.
5 It's exciting to see a lion in the nature.
6 Lay down and be quiet!
7 They showed the Cologne-Leverkusen play on television.
8 Bayern Munich is winning: one – two.
9 That big hole in the road is a really danger!
10 We are fifty in the sports club.
11 Is your woman coming to the party, too?
12 There were forty womans in the club.
13 The secretary cooks coffee in our office.
14 I saw all that happened.
15 The film lasts one and a half hour.
16 I drink often tea in the evening.
17 What does he after work?
18 222 = two hundred twenty-two.
19 He bought a cake to eat it.
20 The kiosk is direct at the entrance.
21 We want to visit Israel on Easter.

22 Her English knowledges could be better.
23 My boss becomes twice as much money as I do.
24 What's with a glass of wine?
25 What colour have the doors?
26 What was the temperature in the shadow?
27 There are two hundred persons in my tennis club.
28 The kidnapper was catched by a private detective.
29 He was angry to go into the dark cellar.
30 They should build a wider street between Bonn and Cologne.

1 "Must you go so early?" – "No, I **needn't**." (94)

2 Is there **room** in your flat for fifty guests? (74)

3 He looked **drunk**. (86)

4 **Everybody** here **is** French. (91)

5 It's exciting to see a lion in the **wild**. (88)

6 **Lie** down and be quiet! (82)

7 They showed the Cologne-Leverkusen **game** on television. (75)

8 Bayern Munich is winning: **two – one**. (73)

9 That big hole in the road is a **real** danger! (71)

10 **There** are fifty **of us** in the sports club. (96)

11 Is your **wife** coming to the party, too? (67)

12 There were forty **women** in the club. (182)

13 The secretary **makes** coffee in our office. (240)

14 I saw **everything** that happened. (92)

15 The film lasts one and a half **hours**. (81)

16 I **often** drink tea in the evening. (85)

17 What **does** he **do** after work? (80)

18 222 = two hundred **and** twenty-two. (70)

19 He bought a cake to **eat**. (44)

20 The kiosk is **right** at the entrance. (89)

21 We want to visit Israel **at** Easter. (93)

22 Her **English** could be better. (69)

23 My boss **gets** twice as much money as I do. (68)

24 **What about** a glass of wine? (87)

25 What colour **are** the doors? (83)

26 What was the temperature in the **shade**? (76)

27 There are two hundred **people** in my tennis club. (84)

28 The kidnapper was **caught** by a private detective. (72)

29 He was **afraid** to go into the dark cellar. (78)

30 They should build a wider **road** between Bonn and Cologne. (77)

1 There's a nice street between the two cities.
2 I always cook coffee in the morning.
3 All photos were taken by my father.
4 Have you got place in your flat for a second child?
5 My seat was direct next to the exit.
6 What's with a game of tennis?
7 You drive always too fast.
8 What colour has gold?
9 All things on the table are mine.
10 The boy was angry to show his father his test results.
11 The temperature was never lower than thirty degrees in the shadow.
12 How many are you in the class?
13 There are two mens from the Post Office at the door.
14 I don't like him and I don't like her, too.
15 She doesn't want beer – she wants something other.
16 The radio report lasted one and a half hour.
17 All people here can speak English.
18 We spent two days in Mainz on Whitsun.
19 Have you ever seen a tiger in the nature?
20 I wasn't drunken yesterday.
21 Twenty persons came to my last party.
22 Henry always lays down when he's tired.
23 What do they in the office?
24 In former times I lived in London.
25 Monopoly is a good play for children.
26 She bought a coke to drink it.
27 (At a petrol station) Can you prove the oil, please?
28 Bonn is nearby Cologne.
29 The dinner cooks my wife.
30 I drive a lot in my job, but I mustn't pay for the petrol.

1 There's a nice **road** between the two cities. (77)

2 I always **make** coffee in the morning. (240)

3 All **the** photos were taken by my father. (98)

4 Have you got **room** in your flat for a second child? (74)

5 My seat was **right** next to the exit. (89)

6 **What about** a game of tennis? (87)

7 You **always** drive too fast. (85)

8 What colour **is** gold? (83)

9 **Everything** on the table **is** mine. (92)

10 The boy was **afraid** to show his father his test results. (78)

11 The temperature was never lower than thirty degrees in the **shade**. (76)

12 How many **of you** are **there** in the class? (96)

13 There are two **men** from the Post Office at the door. (182)

14 I don't like him and I don't like her, **either**. (103)

15 She doesn't want beer – she wants something **different**. (99)

16 The radio report lasted one and a half **hours**. (81)

17 **Everybody** here can speak English. (91)

18 We spent two days in Mainz **at** Whitsun. (93)

19 Have you ever seen a tiger in the **wild**? (88)

20 I wasn't **drunk** yesterday. (86)

21 Twenty **people** came to my last party. (84)

22 Henry always **lies** down when he's tired. (82)

23 What **do** they **do** in the office? (80)

24 I **used to live** in London. (102)

25 Monopoly is a good **game** for children. (75)

26 She bought a coke to **drink**. (44)

27 (At a petrol station) Can you **check** the oil, please? (104)

28 Bonn is **near** Cologne. (101)

29 **My wife cooks** the dinner. (97)

30 I drive a lot in my job, but I **needn't** pay for the petrol. (94)

1 The boss opened the door by himself.
2 He always shaves himself before breakfast.
3 He's been married with Susan for ten years.
4 All glasses are on the table.
5 I live nearby the church.
6 I mean biscuits – cake is something other.
7 You mustn't take your umbrella – it's not raining.
8 Do you always cook coffee after dinner?
9 All people in the office are very nice.
10 It was a shock to see an elephant in the nature.
11 He plays never poker.
12 Three persons died in the fire.
13 I normally lay down for a rest in the afternoon.
14 My brother has four childrens.
15 As child I could run very fast.
16 It was a long travel.
17 He gave us a lot of useful informations.
18 Would you prove the tyre pressure, please?
19 The grass cuts my son.
20 In former times people were happier.
21 We are ten here at the moment.
22 I always stay at home on Christmas.
23 All things in the flat were stolen.
24 The policeman was standing direct next to me.
25 What's with a visit to the zoo?
26 Jim got drunken last Christmas.
27 What colour has snow?
28 She bought a woollen coat to wear it in the winter.
29 They don't drink beer and they don't drink wine, too.
30 This machine you can see in the kitchen.

1 The boss opened the door **himself**. (110)
2 He always **shaves** before breakfast. (107)
3 He's been married **to** Susan for ten years. (105)
4 All **the** glasses are on the table. (98)
5 I live **near** the church. (101)
6 I mean biscuits – cake is something **else**. (99)
7 You **needn't** take your umbrella – it's not raining. (94)
8 Do you always **make** coffee after dinner? (240)
9 **Everybody** in the office **is** very nice. (91)
10 It was a shock to see an elephant in the **wild**. (88)
11 He **never** plays poker. (85)
12 Three **people** died in the fire. (84)
13 I normally **lie** down for a rest in the afternoon. (82)
14 My brother has four **children**. (182)
15 As **a** child I could run very fast. (108)
16 It was a long **trip**. (111)
17 He gave us a lot of useful **information**. (106)
18 Would you **check** the tyre pressure, please? (104)
19 **My son cuts** the grass. (97)
20 People **used to be** happier. (102)
21 **There** are ten **of us** here at the moment. (96)
22 I always stay at home **at** Christmas. (93)
23 **Everything** in the flat **was** stolen. (92)
24 The policeman was standing **right** next to me. (89)
25 **What about** a visit to the zoo? (87)
26 Jim got **drunk** last Christmas. (86)
27 What colour **is** snow? (83)
28 She bought a woollen coat to **wear** in the winter. (44)
29 They don't drink beer and they don't drink wine, **either**. (103)
30 **You can see** this machine in the kitchen. (109)

36 'HORROR' MISTAKES

1 You mustn't learn Japanese – most of them speak English.
2 All things here belong to Susan.
3 What did you do on Christmas?
4 My wife cooks coffee every morning.
5 How many are you at home?
6 The station is nearby the football ground.
7 How long has she been married with Tom?
8 I normally dress myself after breakfast.
9 In former times women didn't wear trousers.
10 These people you can hear on the radio.
11 They went in the opera yesterday.
12 The boss is always crying at us.
13 In the house are seven rooms.
14 It's not plastic – it's something other.
15 The food buys my wife.
16 I know all people here.
17 All cars here were made in Germany.
18 As child she was beautiful.
19 A house animal can be a problem.
20 When did you last prove your blood pressure?
21 The informations he gave us are not correct.
22 Thousand is ten times more than hundred.
23 I didn't really want to make the travel.
24 The boss made the coffee by herself.
25 You mustn't smoke during they are playing.
26 She told that she had a new job.
27 They needed two hours to drive home.
28 Real mens don't cry!
29 They hired a video film to watch it.
30 She doesn't speak Spanish and she doesn't speak Italian, too.

1 You **needn't** learn Japanese – most of them speak English. (94)
2 **Everything** here **belongs** to Susan. (92)
3 What did you do **at** Christmas? (93)
4 My wife **makes** coffee every morning. (240)
5 How many **of you** are **there** at home? (96)
6 The station is **near** the football ground. (101)
7 How long has she been married **to** Tom? (105)
8 I normally **get dressed** after breakfast. (107)
9 Women didn't **use to wear** trousers. (102)
10 **You can hear** these people on the radio. (109)
11 They went **to** the opera yesterday. (112)
12 The boss is always **shouting** at us. (113)
13 **There are** seven rooms in the house. (116)
14 It's not plastic – it's something **different**. (99)
15 **My wife buys** the food. (97)
16 I know **everybody** here. (91)
17 All **the** cars here were made in Germany. (98)
18 As **a** child she was beautiful. (108)
19 A **pet** can be a problem. (119)
20 When did you last **check** your blood pressure? (104)
21 The **information** he gave us **is** not correct. (106)
22 **A** thousand is ten times more than a hundred. (120)
23 I didn't really want to make the **trip**. (111)
24 The boss made the coffee **herself**. (110)
25 You mustn't smoke **while** they are playing. (118)
26 She **said** that she had a new job. (114)
27 **It took them** two hours to drive home. (115)
28 Real **men** don't cry! (182)
29 They hired a video film to **watch**. (44)
30 She doesn't speak Spanish and she doesn't speak Italian, **either**. (103)

1 Mein Bruder hat vier Kinder.
2 Er kaufte sich ein Buch, um es zu lesen.
3 Ich mag alle Leute im Club.
4 Er hat alles mitgenommen.
5 Wir sind zu Weihnachten nach Ungarn gefahren.
6 „Müssen Sie früh aufstehen?“ – „Nein, muß ich nicht.“
7 Ich habe gerade Kaffee gekocht.
8 Wir sind zu zweit hier.
9 Die Arbeit macht mein Sohn.
10 Alle Tassen waren voll.
11 “Ist das Holz?” – “Nein, es ist etwas anderes.”
12 Dover ist in der Nähe von Folkestone.
13 Früher haben die Leute mehr gearbeitet.
14 Ich esse kein Fleisch, und Fisch esse ich auch nicht.
15 Können Sie bitte die Testergebnisse prüfen?
16 Sie ist mit ihm verheiratet.
17 Wir bekamen die Informationen aus Frankreich.
18 Der Junge wäscht sich immer vor dem Frühstück.
19 Als Kind lebte er in Spanien.
20 Den Film können wir morgen sehen.
21 Der Chef hat den Brief selbst getippt.
22 Es war eine interessante Reise.
23 Sie geht mittags immer ins Restaurant.
24 „Raus!“ schrie er mich an.
25 Er sagt immer, daß er kein Geld hat.
26 Ich brauchte eine Stunde, um den Brief zu übersetzen.
27 In dem Gebäude sind vier Wohnungen.
28 Du darfst nicht sprechen, während sie schläft.
29 Haustiere sind wichtig für Kinder.
30 Tausend ist mehr als hundert.

1 My brother has four children. (182)
2 He bought a book to read. (44)
3 I like everybody in the club. (91)
4 He's taken everything with him. (92)
5 We drove to Hungary at Christmas. (93)
6 "Do you have to get up early?" – "No, I don't." (94)
7 I've just made coffee. (240)
8 There are two of us here. (96)
9 My son does the work. (97)
10 All the cups were full. (98)
11 "Is that wood?" – "No, it's something else." (99)
12 Dover is near Folkestone. (101)
13 People used to work more. (102)
14 I don't eat meat, and I don't eat fish, either. (103)
15 Can you check the test results, please? (104)
16 She's married to him. (105)
17 We got the information from France. (106)
18 The boy always gets washed before breakfast. (107)
19 As a child he lived in Spain. (108)
20 We can see the film tomorrow. (109)
21 The boss typed the letter himself. (110)
22 It was an interesting trip. (111)
23 She always goes to the restaurant at lunch-time. (112)
24 "Get out!" he shouted at me. (113)
25 He always says that he has no money. (114)
26 It took me an hour to translate the letter. (115)
27 There are four flats in the building. (116)
28 You mustn't speak while she is sleeping. (118)
29 Pets are important for children. (119)
30 A thousand is more than a hundred. (120)

1 He went in a pub to drink a beer.
2 In former times people had fewer problems.
3 The boss cried at his secretary.
4 How long will you need to come here on Saturday?
5 In this building are twenty-two offices.
6 You must concentrate during you are driving.
7 There are about hundred people in our squash club.
8 You said me you needed help.
9 Do you have any house animals?
10 Have you paid the beer?
11 I searched my book.
12 I couldn't sleep this night.
13 My friend and I we drove to Frankfurt yesterday.
14 I speak a little bit English.
15 Is Berlin bigger as Frankfurt?
16 Take your feets off the table!
17 A house is a thing which you live in it.
18 All books were written by Hemingway.
19 The housework does my daughter.
20 He works nearby my office.
21 It wasn't spaghetti – it was something other.
22 She organised the travel alone.
23 Is he married with Joan?
24 You should prove the spare tyre before the holiday.
25 The young man washed himself before leaving the house.
26 He isn't right, but she isn't right, too.
27 Where can I find the informations?
28 As child he was brilliant.
29 The president gave the speech by himself.
30 That man I saw on television yesterday.

1 He went **to** a pub to drink a beer. (112)
2 People **used to have** fewer problems. (102)
3 The boss **shouted** at his secretary. (113)
4 How long will **it take you** to come here on Saturday? (115)
5 **There are** twenty-two offices in this building. (116)
6 You must concentrate **while** you are driving. (118)
7 There are about **a** hundred people in our squash club. (120)
8 You **told** me you needed help. (114)
9 Do you have any **pets**? (119)
10 Have you paid **for** the beer? (121)
11 I searched **for** my book. (122)
12 I couldn't sleep **last** night. (123)
13 **My friend and I drove** to Frankfurt yesterday. (126)
14 I speak **a little** English. (124)
15 Is Berlin bigger **than** Frankfurt? (125)
16 Take your **feet** off the table! (182)
17 A house is a thing which you **live in**. (44)
18 All **the** books were written by Hemingway. (98)
19 **My daughter does** the housework. (97)
20 He works **near** my office. (101)
21 It wasn't spaghetti – it was something **else**. (99)
22 She organised the **trip** alone. (111)
23 Is he married **to** Joan? (105)
24 You should **check** the spare tyre before the holiday. (104)
25 The young man **washed** before leaving the house. (107)
26 He isn't right, but she isn't right, **either**. (103)
27 Where can I find the **information**? (106)
28 As **a** child he was brilliant. (108)
29 The president gave the speech **himself**. (110)
30 **I saw** that man on television yesterday. (109)

1 The boss typed the letter by himself.
2 The patient told that he had a headache.
3 Did they send the match on television?
4 My son got a good note in German last year.
5 That letter I read yesterday.
6 It was an expensive travel.
7 Which hospital is she lying in?
8 Put off your glove before you shake hands.
9 Johnny, dress yourself! It's time for school!
10 A dress is a thing which a woman wears it.
11 He drank two beers during watching the game.
12 He must drive to Stuttgart last Saturday.
13 The teacher cried at the children.
14 As child you were impossible!
15 The teacher searched her book.
16 He understands a little bit French.
17 How did you sleep this night?
18 She needed an hour to do the work.
19 I haven't paid my coffee yet.
20 John and his wife they are friends of ours.
21 Would you like a glass beer?
22 These informations are for your ears only.

23 In a football team are eleven players.
24 Hundred pfennigs make a mark.
25 The Rhine is longer as the Ahr.
26 She's married with an Englishman.
27 I must go into the supermarket tomorrow.
28 House animals are forbidden in our block of flats.
29 "Who's winning?" – "Cologne, three to one."
30 He told the childrens to be quiet.

1 The boss typed the letter **himself**. (110)
2 The patient **said** that he had a headache. (114)
3 Did they **show** the match on television? (129)
4 My son got a good **mark** in German last year. (132)
5 **I read** that letter yesterday. (109)
6 It was an expensive **trip**. (111)
7 Which hospital **is** she in? (133)
8 **Take off** your glove before you shake hands. (131)
9 Johnny, **get dressed**! It's time for school! (107)
10 A dress is a thing which a woman **wears**. (44)
11 He drank two beers **while** watching the game. (118)
12 He **had to** drive to Stuttgart last Saturday. (130)
13 The teacher **shouted** at the children. (113)
14 As **a** child you were impossible! (108)
15 The teacher **looked for** her book. (122)
16 He understands **a little** French. (124)
17 How did you sleep **last** night? (123)
18 **It took her** an hour to do the work. (115)
19 I haven't paid **for** my coffee yet. (121)
20 **John and his wife are** friends of ours. (126)
21 Would you like a glass **of** beer? (127)
22 **This information is** for your ears only. (106)
23 **There are** eleven players in a football club. (116)
24 **A** hundred pfennigs make a mark. (120)
25 The Rhine is longer **than** the Ahr. (125)
26 She's married **to** an Englishman. (105)
27 I must go **to** the supermarket tomorrow. (112)
28 **Pets** are forbidden in our block of flats. (119)
29 "Who's winning?" – "Cologne, **three-one**." (128)
30 He told the **children** to be quiet. (182)

1 He must drive to Hamburg last Friday.
2 Johnny, take off the dirty shoes!
3 How many mistakes did you do in the test?
4 We understand a little bit Italian.
5 Hundred pence make a pound.
6 "Who can write the report?" – "I do it!"
7 Cheese is made of milk.
8 You should put off your thick pullover when you play tennis.
9 Tom and Bob they are good players.
10 I woke up at three thirty this night.
11 You are not allowed to have house animals here.
12 Don't talk during your father is talking!
13 The fans didn't stop crying for ninety minutes.
14 They seldom send opera on television.
15 The little boy searched his money.
16 "Who's winning?" – "Stuttgart, two to one."
17 You look bad – what have you?
18 He said me he was unhappy.
19 Let the boy alone!
20 What kind of note did your daughter get in history?
21 He hasn't paid the car yet.
22 Mary is smaller as Jane.
23 Rolls Royce shall be the best car in the world.
24 There were four womans in the shop.
25 We went in the restaurant early.
26 My brother is lying in hospital at the moment.
27 Can you give me a glass water, please?
28 They needed three days to finish the job.
29 Football is a game which men normally play it.
30 In the city are twenty-one cinemas.

1 He **had to** drive to Hamburg last Friday. (130)
2 Johnny, take off **your** dirty shoes! (138)
3 How many mistakes did you **make** in the test? (137)
4 We understand **a little** Italian. (124)
5 **A** hundred pence make a pound. (120)
6 "Who can write the report?" – "**I'll** do it!" (140)
7 Cheese is made **from** milk. (135)
8 You should **take off** your thick pullover when you play tennis. (131)
9 **Tom and Bob are** good players. (126)
10 I woke up at three thirty **last** night. (123)
11 You are not allowed to have **pets** here. (119)
12 Don't talk **while** your father is talking! (118)
13 The fans didn't stop **shouting** for ninety minutes. (113)
14 They seldom **show** opera on television. (129)
15 The little boy **looked for** his money. (122)
16 "Who's winning?" – "Stuttgart, **two-one**." (128)
17 You look bad – **what's wrong with you**? (136)
18 He **told** me he was unhappy. (114)
19 **Leave** the boy alone! (134)
20 What kind of **mark** did your daughter get in history? (132)
21 He hasn't paid **for** the car yet. (121)
22 Mary is smaller **than** Jane. (125)
23 Rolls Royce **is supposed to** be the best car in the world. (139)
24 There were four **women** in the shop. (182)
25 We went **to** the restaurant early. (112)
26 My brother **is** in hospital at the moment. (133)
27 Can you give me a glass **of** water, please? (127)
28 **It took them** three days to finish the job. (115)
29 Football is a game which men normally **play**. (44)
30 **There are** twenty-one cinemas in the city. (116)

1 They should send more hockey on television.
2 John has been lying in hospital for two weeks.
3 You had right – it is colder today!
4 I must phone Susan yesterday.
5 She had a small hat on the head.
6 He searched his key.
7 The garage is made from concrete.
8 The bird broke his wing.
9 "Who can help Susan?" – "I help her."
10 Beer is a drink which Germans like it.
11 They learnt a little bit Italian.
12 Are the beers paid?
13 Don't forget to buy a kilo sugar!
14 He was dressed with a blazer.
15 I'm lighter as you.

16 Porsche shall be the fastest German car.
17 You should put off your hat when you meet a lady.
18 Uwe got a better note in French than in English.
19 Take your hands out of the pockets!
20 How many womens are there in the club?
21 Oh, go away, and let us alone!
22 He sat before the television.
23 "Who's winning?" – "Munich, four to nil."
24 He looks unhappy! What has he?
25 The trains arrived all two minutes.
26 I was awake all night this night.
27 The goalkeeper did a terrible mistake in the final.
28 Joan and I we are just good friends.
29 "How much overtime do the men work?" – "That's different."
30 The sixth of April, nineteen hundred and eighty-one = 6/4/1981

1 They should **show** more hockey on television. (129)
2 John **has been** in hospital for two weeks. (133)
3 You **were** right – it is colder today! (147)
4 I **had to** phone Susan yesterday. (130)
5 She had a small hat on **her** head. (142)
6 He searched **for** his key. (122)
7 The garage is made **of** concrete. (135)
8 The bird broke **its** wing. (143)
9 "Who can help Susan?" – "I'**ll** help her." (140)
10 Beer is a drink which Germans **like**. (44)
11 They learnt **a little** Italian. (124)
12 Are the beers paid **for**? (121)
13 Don't forget to buy a kilo **of** sugar! (127)
14 He was dressed **in** a blazer. (145)
15 I'm lighter **than** you. (125)
16 Porsche **is supposed to** be the fastest German car. (139)
17 You should **take off** your hat when you meet a lady. (131)
18 Uwe got a better **mark** in French than in English. (132)
19 Take your hands out of **your** pockets! (138)
20 How many **women** are there in the club? (182)
21 Oh, go away, and **leave** us alone! (134)
22 He sat **in front of** the television. (141)
23 "Who's winning?" – "Munich, **four-nil**." (128)
24 He looks unhappy! **What's wrong with him**? (136)
25 The trains arrived **every** two minutes. (144)
26 I was awake all night **last** night. (123)
27 The goalkeeper **made** a terrible mistake in the final. (137)
28 **Joan and I are** just good friends. (126)
29 "How much overtime do the men work?" – "**It varies**." (148)
30 The sixth of April, **nineteen eighty-one** = 6/4/1981 (146)

1 Kinder machen viel Lärm.
2 Er kaufte sich einen Ball, um damit zu spielen.
3 Ich habe das Bier schon bezahlt.
4 Der Junge suchte seinen Ball.
5 Ich habe heute nacht schlecht geschlafen.
6 Sie spricht sehr wenig Englisch.
7 Sein Büro ist größer als meins.
8 Ihr Mann und ich spielen in demselben Verein.
9 Möchtest du eine Tasse Tee?
10 FC Köln führt drei zu eins.
11 Heute abend senden sie Tennis live.
12 Wir mußten gestern Überstunden machen.
13 Zieh die schmutzigen Schuhe aus!
14 Ulrike kriegt immer eine gute Note in Mathe.
15 Er lag drei Wochen im Krankenhaus.
16 Laß den Jungen in Ruhe!
17 Butter wird aus Milch gemacht.
18 Sie sieht krank aus – was hat sie?
19 Ich habe einen großen Fehler gemacht.
20 Sie zog den Mantel aus und setzte sich hin.
21 Morgen soll es schneien.
22 „Wer wird mir morgen meinen Brief tippen?“ – „Ich!“
23 Er parkte sein Auto vor dem Kino.
24 Sie hatte einen Ring am Finger.
25 Die Katze putzte sich die Ohren.
26 Die Flugzeuge starten alle zehn Minuten.
27 Die Dame war mit einem teuren Mantel bekleidet.
28 Der Krieg endete neunzehnhundertfünfundvierzig.
29 Sie haben recht.
30 „Wann kommt er nach Hause?“ – „Das ist unterschiedlich.“

1 Children make a lot of noise. (182)
2 He bought a ball to play with. (44)
3 I've already paid for the beer. (121)
4 The boy looked for his ball. (122)
5 I slept badly last night. (123)
6 She speaks very little English. (124)
7 His office is bigger than mine. (125)
8 Her husband and I play in the same club. (126)
9 Would you like a cup of tea? (127)
10 FC Cologne is leading three – one. (128)
11 They're showing tennis live tonight. (129)
12 We had to do overtime yesterday. (130)
13 Take your dirty shoes off! (131)
14 Ulrike always gets a good mark in maths. (132)
15 He was in hospital for three weeks. (133)
16 Leave the boy alone! (134)
17 Butter is made from milk. (135)
18 She looks ill – what's wrong with her? (136)
19 I've made a big mistake. (137)
20 She took off her coat and sat down. (138)
21 It's supposed to snow tomorrow. (139)
22 "Who will type my letter for me tomorrow?" – "I will!" (140)
23 He parked his car in front of the cinema. (141)
24 She had a ring on her finger. (142)
25 The cat washed its ears. (143)
26 The planes take off every ten minutes. (144)
27 The lady was dressed in an expensive coat. (145)
28 The war ended in nineteen forty-five. (146)
29 You are right. (147)
30 "When does he get home?" – "It varies." (148)

1 He was looking to himself in the mirror.
2 "Who's winning?" – "Bremen, three to two."
3 What time did they send the tennis yesterday?
4 We fly to Spain each year.
5 We painted the sleeping-room last month.
6 Won't you take off the hat?
7 Have you something? You don't look well.
8 "Who wants to play tennis tomorrow?" – "I play!"
9 What shall the weather be like tomorrow?
10 The cat injured her leg.
11 I did a lot of mistakes in the test yesterday.
12 He looks like an ill man.
13 The planes landed all five minutes.
14 They were dressed with uniforms.
15 "How many cups of tea do you drink a day?" – "That's different."
16 She got a good note from the French teacher.
17 You're Italian! Have I right?
18 I visited this school for five years.
19 They must do overtime yesterday.
20 How is the weather like today?
21 I'd like a litre milk, please.
22 I saw three womens in the car.
23 Let me alone!
24 I don't like lying in hospital.
25 Where's the next post-office?
26 Yoghurt is made of milk.
27 She's sitting before the window.

28 He wore tennis shoes on the feet.
29 The seventh of May, nineteen hundred sixty-six = 7/5/1966
30 You should put off your T-shirt before you go into the water.

1 He was looking **at** himself in the mirror. (100)

2 "Who's winning?" – "Bremen, **three-two**." (128)

3 What time did they **show** the tennis yesterday? (129)

4 We fly to Spain **every** year. (154)

5 We painted the **bedroom** last month. (153)

6 Won't you take off **your** hat? (138)

7 **Is something wrong with you**? You don't look well. (136)

8 "Who wants to play tennis tomorrow?" – "I'**ll** play!" (140)

9 What'**s** the weather **supposed to** be like tomorrow? (139)

10 The cat injured **its** leg. (143)

11 I **made** a lot of mistakes in the test yesterday. (137)

12 He looks like **a sick** man. (149)

13 The planes landed **every** five minutes. (144)

14 They were dressed **in** uniforms. (145)

15 "How many cups of tea do you drink a day?" –
"**It depends**." (148)

16 She got a good **mark** from the French teacher. (132)

17 You're Italian! **Am** I right? (147)

18 I **went to** this school for five years. (150)

19 They **had to** do overtime yesterday. (130)

20 **What** is the weather like today? (151)

21 I'd like a litre **of** milk, please. (127)

22 I saw three **women** in the car. (182)

23 **Leave** me alone! (134)

24 I don't like **being** in hospital. (133)

25 Where's the **nearest** post-office? (152)

26 Yoghurt is made **from** milk. (135)

27 She's sitting **in front of** the window. (141)

28 He wore tennis shoes on **his** feet. (142)

29 The seventh of May, **nineteen sixty-six** = 7/5/1966 (146)

30 You should **take off** your T-shirt before you go into the water. (131)

1 She was dressed with a fur coat.
2 We made holidays in Spain last year.
3 We play tennis each week.
4 Do you know where the next hospital is?
5 I'm interested for football.
6 The man have no money.
7 "What time do you usually get up?" – "That's different."
8 He was by his mother yesterday.
9 Just look to the Jaguar – another fine English car!
10 Swimming shall be the best kind of sport.
11 The flat has only two sleeping-rooms.
12 His wife is a very ill woman.
13 They had gloves on the hands.
14 She looks unhappy – what has she?
15 He'd like an own flat.
16 The dog always eats his food too fast.
17 Let the children alone!
18 Think on me when I'm away!
19 Come in – give me the coat.
20 The tenth of June, fourteen hundred and ninety-two = 10/6/1492
21 The player didn't do any mistakes in the game.
22 She has right – it really is a hard job.
23 How was the match like yesterday?
24 We visited the theatre last night.
25 The buses ran all twenty minutes.
26 Two womens live in the house.
27 What's your meaning?
28 I saw them standing before the house.
29 The chair is made from wood.
30 "Who would like to help?" – "I help!"

1 She was dressed **in** a fur coat. (145)
2 We **spent our** holidays in Spain last year. (158)
3 We play tennis **every** week. (154)
4 Do you know where the **nearest** hospital is? (152)
5 I'm interested **in** football. (161)
6 The man **has** no money. (155)
7 "What time do you usually get up?" – "**It depends**." (148)
8 He was **at** his mother**'s** yesterday. (157)
9 Just look **at** the Jaguar – another fine English car! (100)
10 Swimming **is supposed to** be the best kind of sport. (139)
11 The flat has only two **bedrooms**. (153)
12 His wife is a very **sick** woman. (149)
13 They had gloves on **their** hands. (142)
14 She looks unhappy – **what's wrong with her**? (136)
15 He'd like **his** own flat. (156)
16 The dog always eats **its** food too fast. (143)
17 **Leave** the children alone! (134)
18 Think **about** me when I'm away! (160)
19 Come in – give me **your** coat. (138)
20 The tenth of June, **fourteen ninety-two** = 10/6/1492 (146)
21 The player didn't **make** any mistakes in the game. (137)
22 She **is** right – it really is a hard job. (147)
23 **What** was the match like yesterday? (151)
24 We **went to** the theatre last night. (150)
25 The buses ran **every** twenty minutes. (144)
26 Two **women** live in the house. (182)
27 What's your **opinion**? (159)
28 I saw them standing **in front of** the house. (141)
29 The chair is made **of** wood. (135)
30 "Who would like to help?" – "**I'll** help!" (140)

1 How is your boss like?
2 He was dressed with a blue raincoat.
3 They lived in Hamburg in the eighty years.
4 She's interested for badminton.
5 If they don't come until five, we'll begin without them.
6 I like to make holidays in July.
7 I met him on the airport.
8 Who's standing before the door?
9 The next pub is round the corner.
10 I have something in the eye.
11 I've got an own car.
12 I had right – England won the World Cup in '66!
13 You can take all what you can carry.
14 I think it won't rain tomorrow.
15 Trains to Bonn run all two hours.
16 The fish opened his mouth.
17 This is my meaning.
18 John is an ill child.
19 Think on our wonderful holiday last year!
20 The ninth of July, nineteen hundred eighty-three = 9/7/1983
21 He have no time.
22 I visited this school for a long time.
23 "Can you speak more clearly, please?" – "I'll try it."
24 Which is my sleeping-room?
25 Just look for Tom – he's standing on his head!
26 "What do you usually do at the weekend?" – "That's different."
27 She's by the baker.
28 He's got big feets.
29 Remember me to take my medicine, please.
30 They have a holiday each summer.

1 **What** is your boss like? (151)

2 He was dressed **in** a blue raincoat. (145)

3 They lived in Hamburg in the **eighties**. (166)

4 She's interested **in** badminton. (161)

5 If they don't come **by** five, we'll begin without them. (164)

6 I like to **have my** holidays in July. (158)

7 I met him **at** the airport. (167)

8 Who's standing **in front of** the door? (141)

9 The **nearest** pub is round the corner. (152)

10 I have something in **my** eye. (142)

11 I've got **a car of my own**. (156)

12 I **was** right – England won the World Cup in '66! (147)

13 You can take **everything** you can carry. (162)

14 I **don't think** it **will rain** tomorrow. (168)

15 Trains to Bonn run **every** two hours. (144)

16 The fish opened **its** mouth. (143)

17 This is my **opinion**. (159)

18 John is **a sick** child. (149)

19 Think **about** our wonderful holiday last year! (160)

20 The ninth of July, **nineteen eighty-three** = 9/7/1983 (146)

21 He **has** no time. (155)

22 I **went to** this school for a long time. (150)

23 "Can you speak more clearly, please?" – "I'**ll** try." (163)

24 Which is my **bedroom**? (153)

25 Just look **at** Tom – he's standing on his head! (100)

26 "What do you usually do at the weekend?" – "**It depends**." (148)

27 She's **at** the baker**'s**. (157)

28 He's got big **feet**. (182)

29 **Remind** me to take my medicine, please. (165)

30 They have a holiday **every** summer. (154)

1 He is by the hairdresser.
2 They has to work today.
3 I arrived at home late yesterday.
4 The sun raises early in the summer.
5 He's interested for languages.
6 We met our business colleagues on the fair.
7 When is your neighbour making holidays?
8 The boy's very ill – the doctor's looking for him.
9 Explain me the problem.
10 Think on the good old times!
11 Remember me to phone them, please.
12 We have to paint the sleeping-room.
13 Carol visits the best school in the city.
14 Where were you in the sixty years?
15 I think the winter won't be bad.
16 She has an own firm.
17 He heard all what we said.
18 I always go home after the work.

19 How was the party like last Friday?
20 My feets are killing me!
21 She's a very ill girl.
22 "Can you speak a bit louder, please?" – "I'll try it."
23 What's the boss's meaning?
24 Can you borrow me this book, please?
25 I went to the bed early last night.
26 Tom goes to the mountains each winter.
27 Germany had economical problems after the war.
28 If you haven't finished until two, you'll get no money.
29 The next supermarket is in King street.
30 What do you normally do at noon?

1 He is **at** the hairdresser**'s**. (157)
2 They **have** to work today. (155)
3 I **arrived home** late yesterday. (176)
4 The sun **rises** early in the summer. (173)
5 He's interested **in** languages. (161)
6 We met our business colleagues **at** the fair. (167)
7 When is your neighbour **going on holiday**? (158)
8 The boy's very ill – the doctor's looking **after** him. (100)
9 Explain the problem **to me**. (175)
10 Think **about** the good old times! (160)
11 **Remind** me to phone them, please. (165)
12 We have to paint the **bedroom**. (153)
13 Carol **goes to** the best school in the city. (150)
14 Where were you in the **sixties**? (166)
15 I **don't think** the winter **will be** bad. (168)
16 She has **her** own firm. (156)
17 He heard **everything** we said. (162)
18 I always go home **after work**. (169)
19 **What** was the party like last Friday? (151)
20 My **feet** are killing me! (182)
21 She's a very **sick** girl. (149)
22 "Can you speak a bit louder, please?" – "**I'll try.**" (163)
23 What's the boss's **opinion**? (159)
24 Can you **lend** me this book, please? (172)
25 I went **to bed** early last night. (171)
26 Tom goes to the mountains **every** winter. (154)
27 Germany had **economic** problems after the war. (174)
28 If you haven't finished **by** two, you'll get no money. (164)
29 The **nearest** supermarket is in King street. (152)
30 What do you normally do at **lunch-time**? (170)

1 Meine Füße bringen mich noch um!
2 Guck dir das mal an!
3 Herr Müller ist ein sehr kranker Mann.
4 Ich besuchte diese Schule bis 1980.
5 Wie war der Film gestern?
6 Wo ist der nächste Supermarkt?
7 Mein Schlafzimmer ist nicht sehr groß.
8 Hier schneit es jedes Jahr.
9 Er hat ein großes Haus in Berlin.
10 Er hat ein eigenes Auto.
11 Ich war gestern beim Arzt.
12 Wir machen dieses Jahr keinen Urlaub.
13 Ist das deine Meinung?
14 Denk an mich, wenn du im Urlaub bist.
15 Ich interessiere mich für alles.
16 Ich sah alles, was Sie gemacht haben.
17 „Können Sie mir helfen?" – „Ich versuche es."
18 Wir müssen bis Mitternacht damit fertig sein.
19 Erinnere mich daran, das Licht auszumachen.
20 Ich verbrachte die sechziger Jahre in Spanien.
21 Wir sehen uns morgen auf der Messe.
22 Ich glaube, sie wird es nicht machen.
23 Nach der Arbeit gehen wir immer schwimmen.
24 Mittags kommt mein Mann immer nach Hause.
25 Wir sind gestern früh ins Bett gegangen.
26 Er hat uns das Geld geliehen.
27 Wo geht die Sonne auf?
28 Die wirtschaftliche Lage ist schlecht.
29 Sie erklärte ihm die Lage.
30 Wir sind spät am Flughafen angekommen.

1 My feet are killing me! (182)
2 Just look at that! (100)
3 Mr Müller is a very sick man. (149)
4 I went to this school till 1980. (150)
5 What was the film like yesterday? (151)
6 Where is the nearest supermarket? (152)
7 My bedroom isn't very big. (153)
8 It snows here every year. (154)
9 He's got a big house in Berlin. (155)
10 He's got his own car. (156)
11 I was at the doctor's yesterday. (157)
12 We aren't having a holiday this year. (158)
13 Is that your opinion? (159)
14 Think of me when you are on holiday. (160)
15 I'm interested in everything. (161)
16 I saw everything you did. (162)
17 "Can you help me?" – "I'll try." (163)
18 We must be finished with it by midnight. (164)
19 Remind me to switch off the light. (165)
20 I spent the sixties in Spain. (166)
21 See you at the fair tomorrow. (167)
22 I don't think she will do it. (168)
23 We always go swimming after work. (169)
24 My husband always comes home at lunch-time. (170)
25 We went to bed early yesterday. (171)
26 He lent us the money. (172)
27 Where does the sun rise? (173)
28 The economic situation is bad. (174)
29 She explained the situation to him. (175)
30 We arrived at the airport late. (176)

1 I saw a lot of customers on the fair.
2 The students has no free time.
3 Just look on him – he's crazy!
4 I was by the lawyer yesterday.
5 The country has had economical problems for years.
6 He'll explain us the situation.
7 I like comedians – Woody Allen or so.
8 They saw all what happened.
9 We made no holidays last year.
10 Can you lift the table by your own?
11 If she hasn't done the work until six, I'll fire her.
12 The group made some good records in the seventy years.
13 I think the summer won't be good.
14 We drove yesterday to the city.
15 Childrens can be very noisy.
16 What time did you go to the bed yesterday?
17 They have an own house.
18 He arrived the office late yesterday.
19 Can you borrow me DM 100, please?
20 A fifteen-years-old boy can't do this work.
21 They're interested for sports.
22 I always go for a walk at noon.
23 Rise your hands above your head!
24 Is yours the same than mine?
25 What time do you normally finish the work?
26 We are very lucky together – we've been married for twenty years now!
27 In our meaning we need a new secretary.
28 Think on our last trip to Spain!
29 "Can you lift this table on your own?" – "I'll try it."
30 Remember me to buy my wife a present, please.

1 I saw a lot of customers **at** the fair. (167)
2 The students **have** no free time. (155)
3 Just look **at** him – he's crazy! (100)
4 I was **at** the lawyer**'s** yesterday. (157)
5 The country has had **economic** problems for years. (174)
6 He'll explain the situation **to us**. (175)
7 I like comedians – Woody Allen or **somebody like that**. (180)
8 They saw **everything that** happened. (162)
9 We **didn't have a holiday** last year. (158)
10 Can you lift the table **on** your own? (179)
11 If she hasn't done the work **by** six, I'll fire her. (164)
12 The group made some good records in the **seventies**. (166)
13 I **don't think** the summer **will be** good. (168)
14 We drove to the city **yesterday**. (177)
15 **Children** can be very noisy. (182)
16 What time did you go **to bed** yesterday? (171)
17 They have **their** own house. (156)
18 He arrived **at** the office late yesterday. (176)
19 Can you **lend** me DM 100, please? (172)
20 A fifteen-**year**-old boy can't do this work. (183)
21 They're interested **in** sports. (161)
22 I always go for a walk at **lunch-time**. (170)
23 **Raise** your hands above your head! (173)
24 Is yours the same **as** mine? (178)
25 What time do you normally finish **work**? (169)
26 We are very **happy** together – we've been married for twenty years now! (181)
27 In our **opinion** we need a new secretary. (159)
28 Think **about** our last trip to Spain! (160)
29 "Can you lift this table on your own?" – "**I'll try.**" (163)
30 **Remind** me to buy my wife a present, please. (165)

1 I'm tired – I'm going to the bed.
2 We have to arrive the cinema before seven o'clock.
3 Whisky is an art of alcohol.
4 I think it won't snow tomorrow.
5 "You idiot!" he shouted to me.
6 They are Italian, or?
7 Let's meet on the airport.
8 The commandos ran behind the terrorist.
9 We start the work at eight o'clock.
10 The reporter wrote down all what was said.
11 "Can you carry that box by yourself?" – "I'll try it."
12 Where do you eat at noon?
13 If the bus doesn't come until ten, we'll have to walk.
14 I'll ask Dad if I can lend his car.
15 Just look to them – they're swimming in cold water!
16 Remember me to phone my wife, please.
17 There are four womans in our office.
18 They discussed about the weather for hours.
19 The Monday is the worst day.
20 He wrote all his books in the fifty years.
21 A fourteen-years-old girl painted this picture.
22 Have you got time enough to play a round of golf?
23 What are you so lucky about on Monday morning?
24 They played last week in Munich.
25 They have risen the price of cigarettes again.
26 I can't translate the letter by my own.
27 The economical situation is getting better.
28 She likes dry wines – Chablis or so.
29 Can you explain me what happened?
30 My car isn't the same than yours.

1 I'm tired – I'm going **to bed**. (171)
2 We have to arrive **at** the cinema before seven o'clock. (176)
3 Whisky is **a kind** of alcohol. (189)
4 I **don't think** it **will snow** tomorrow. (168)
5 "You idiot!" he shouted **at** me. (187)
6 They are Italian, **aren't they**? (185)
7 Let's meet **at** the airport. (167)
8 The commandos ran **after** the terrorist. (190)
9 We start **work** at eight o'clock. (169)
10 The reporter wrote down **everything that** was said. (162)
11 "Can you carry that box by yourself?" – "I'**ll try.**" (163)
12 Where do you eat at **lunch-time**? (170)
13 If the bus doesn't come **by** ten, we'll have to walk. (164)
14 I'll ask Dad if I can **borrow** his car. (172)
15 Just look **at** them – they're swimming in cold water! (100)
16 **Remind** me to phone my wife, please. (165)
17 There are four **women** in our office. (182)
18 They **discussed** the weather for hours. (188)
19 **Monday** is the worst day. (186)
20 He wrote all his books in the **fifties**. (166)
21 A fourteen-**year**-old girl painted this picture. (183)
22 Have you got **enough time** to play a round of golf? (184)
23 What are you so **happy** about on Monday morning? (181)
24 They played in Munich **last week**. (177)
25 They have **raised** the price of cigarettes again. (173)
26 I can't translate the letter by **myself**. (179)
27 The **economic** situation is getting better. (174)
28 She likes dry wines – Chablis or **something like that**. (180)
29 Can you explain **to me** what happened? (175)
30 My car isn't the same **as** yours. (178)

1 Did you arrive at home early yesterday?
2 My little car is very economic.
3 My wife was so lucky when our daughter got married.
4 He's got no money – he wants to lend some.
5 Her man is a tyrant at home.
6 I spoke to him at midday yesterday.
7 You can swim, or?
8 I haven't got money enough to finish the work.
9 He goes to school for learning something.
10 The police ran behind the robber.
11 They can't finish the work by their own.
12 Have you ever seen the sun raise above the horizon?
13 He explained us the rules.
14 I make a walk after breakfast every day.
15 They discussed about the situation yesterday.
16 "Didn't you see him?" – "Yes, I didn't."
17 English beer isn't the same than German beer.
18 The womans in the office are very nice.
19 He'd like a fast car – a Porsche or so.
20 I spoke last Friday to the boss.
21 What means "window" in German?
22 She went to the bed after dinner.
23 On the medicine bottle stood, "Not for children!"
24 Do you know what is happened?
25 Chablis is a special art of wine.
26 A six-years-old boy was killed in the accident.
27 Just look for her – she's wearing a mini!
28 The Sunday is the best day.
29 I always finish the work at four in the afternoon.
30 "Idiots!" he shouted to them.

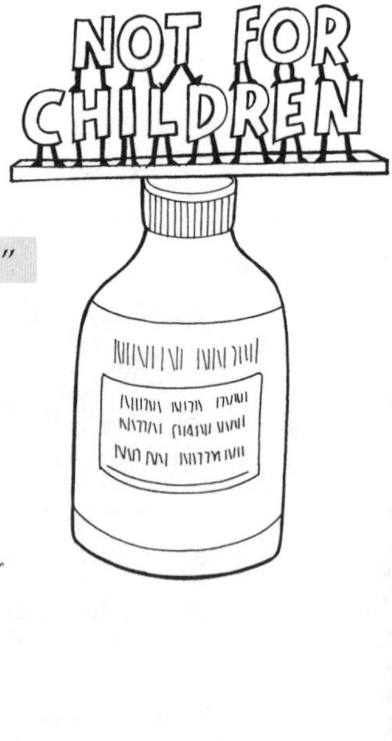

1 Did you **arrive home** early yesterday? (176)
2 My little car is very **economical**. (174)
3 My wife was so **happy** when our daughter got married. (181)
4 He's got no money – he wants to **borrow** some. (172)
5 Her **husband** is a tyrant at home. (195)
6 I spoke to him at **lunch-time** yesterday. (170)
7 You can swim, **can't you**? (185)
8 I haven't got **enough money** to finish the work. (184)
9 He goes to school **to learn** something. (193)
10 The police ran **after** the robber. (190)
11 They can't finish the work **on** their own. (179)
12 Have you ever seen the sun **rise** above the horizon? (173)
13 He explained the rules **to us**. (175)
14 I **go for** a walk after breakfast every day. (191)
15 They **discussed** the situation yesterday. (188)
16 "Didn't you see him?" – "**Yes, I did**." / "**No, I didn't**." (192)
17 English beer isn't the same **as** German beer. (178)
18 The **women** in the office are very nice. (182)
19 He'd like a fast car – a Porsche or **something like that**. (180)
20 I spoke to the boss **last Friday**. (177)
21 What **does** "window" **mean** in German? (194)
22 She went **to bed** after dinner. (171)
23 On the medicine bottle **it said**, "Not for children!" (197)
24 Do you know what **has** happened? (196)
25 Chablis is a special **kind** of wine. (189)
26 A six-**year**-old boy was killed in the accident. (183)
27 Just look **at** her – she's wearing a mini! (100)
28 **Sunday** is the best day. (186)
29 I always finish **work** at four in the afternoon. (169)
30 "Idiots!" he shouted **at** them. (187)

1 I haven't got patience enough to learn to play the piano.
2 I work for earning money.
3 He will go, or?
4 It's not red, but blue.
5 The life is hard.
6 On the poster stood "Pop Music – Tonight !"
7 Have you got anything against a headache?
8 "Nice to see you!" he shouted at me.
9 I ran behind the thief.
10 A seven-years-old girl was the winner.
11 He comes every time late.
12 He doesn't know what is happened.
13 Did you make a walk yesterday?
14 A poodle isn't the same than a boxer.
15 I'm so lucky to see you again!
16 Paella is a special art of Spanish food.
17 They fighted like wild men.
18 Three mens work here in the office.
19 They came yesterday to the office.
20 Don't look to the room – we had a party last night.
21 What means "cat" in German?
22 The Tuesday is a workday.
23 We'll have to discuss about the new system.
24 Her man earns less than she does.
25 "Haven't you eaten?" – "Yes, I haven't."
26 Berlin is a big town.
27 He has ever collected stamps.
28 She'll never manage it by her own.
29 Washing dishes is a work I don't like.
30 I want a holiday in the sun – Spain or so.

1 I haven't got **enough patience** to learn to play the piano. (184)
2 I work **to earn** money. (193)
3 He will go, **won't he**? (185)
4 It's not red, **it's** blue. (204)
5 **Life** is hard. (202)
6 On the poster **it said** "Pop Music – Tonight !" (197)
7 Have you got anything **for** a headache? (200)
8 "Nice to see you!" he shouted **to** me. (187)
9 I ran **after** the thief. (190)
10 A seven-**year**-old girl was the winner. (183)
11 He **always** comes late. (203)
12 He doesn't know what **has** happened. (196)
13 Did you **go for** a walk yesterday? (191)
14 A poodle isn't the same **as** a boxer. (178)
15 I'm so **happy** to see you again! (181)
16 Paella is a special **kind** of Spanish food. (189)
17 They **fought** like wild men. (205)
18 Three **men** work here in the office. (182)
19 They came to the office **yesterday**. (177)
20 Don't look **at** the room – we had a party last night. (100)
21 What **does** "cat" **mean** in German? (194)
22 **Tuesday** is a workday. (186)
23 We'll have to **discuss** the new system. (188)
24 Her **husband** earns less than she does. (195)
25 "Haven't you eaten?" – "**No, I haven't**." / "**Yes, I have**." (192)
26 Berlin is a big **city**. (198)
27 He has **always** collected stamps. (199)
28 She'll never manage it **on** her own. (179)
29 Washing dishes is a **job** I don't like. (201)
30 I want a holiday in the sun – Spain or **somewhere like that**. (180)

1 Drei Frauen arbeiten in diesem Büro.

2 Er muß nach seiner kranken Mutter sehen.

3 Wir trafen gestern Freunde in der Stadt.

4 Das Bild ist das gleiche wie meins.

5 Schaffen Sie es alleine?

6 Ich möchte etwas essen – ein Butterbrot, oder so.

7 Freitags um fünf bin ich immer so glücklich.

8 Ein fünfjähriges Kind könnte das besser machen.

9 Haben Sie Geld genug, um es zu kaufen?

10 Sie ist Spanierin, oder?

11 Der Sonntag ist ein Familientag.

12 „Sie Idiot!" schrie er mich an.

13 Sie können stundenlang über Politik diskutieren.

14 Jogging ist eine Art Sport.

15 Der Polizist lief hinter dem Mörder her.

16 Komm – machen wir einen Spaziergang.

17 „Hast du nichts getrunken?" – „Doch, habe ich."

18 Sie kommt hierher, um Englisch zu lernen.

19 Was heißt „Tisch" auf englisch?

20 Ihr Mann ist sehr nett.

21 Was ist passiert?

22 Auf dem Schild stand „Gefahr".

23 Frankfurt ist eine sehr reiche Stadt.

24 Er hat immer Tennis gespielt.

25 Haben Sie etwas gegen Sonnenbrand?

26 Er hat eine sehr interessante Arbeit.

27 Das Leben kann sehr schön sein.

28 Er kauft jedesmal einen anderen Wein.

29 Es ist nicht Gold, sondern Silber.

30 Die Mannschaft kämpfte bis zum Schluß.

1 Three women work in this office. (182)

2 He must look after his sick mother. (100)

3 We met some friends in the city yesterday. (177)

4 This picture is the same as mine. (178)

5 Can you manage it on your own? (179)

6 I'd like something to eat – a sandwich, or something like that. (180)

7 I'm always so happy at five on Fridays. (181)

8 A five-year-old child could do that better. (183)

9 Do you have enough money to buy it? (184)

10 She is Spanish, isn't she? (185)

11 Sunday is a family day. (186)

12 "You idiot!" he shouted at me. (187)

13 They can discuss politics for hours. (188)

14 Jogging is a kind of sport. (189)

15 The policeman ran after the murderer. (190)

16 Come on – let's go for a walk. (191)

17 "Didn't you drink anything?" – "Yes, I did." (192)

18 She comes here to learn English. (193)

19 What does "Tisch" mean in English? (194)

20 Her husband is very nice. (195)

21 What has happened? (196)

22 On the sign it said "Danger". (197)

23 Frankfurt is a very rich city. (198)

24 He has always played tennis. (199)

25 Have you got anything for sunburn? (200)

26 He's got a very interesting job. (201)

27 Life can be very beautiful. (202)

28 He always buys a different wine. (203)

29 It's not gold, it's silver. (204)

30 The team fought till the end. (205)

1 She has ever collected photos of pop stars.
2 What means "dog" in German?
3 He likes to make a walk in the evening.
4 My jacket has three buttoms.
5 She can type, or?
6 His car is other than ours.
7 I haven't got money enough.
8 This is a very hard work.
9 The time flies.
10 What stands on the back of the book?
11 Where do you know my name from?
12 Munich is a nice town.
13 I need something against headaches.
14 Excuse me for coming late.
15 The dog ran behind the cat.
16 Borussia lost, but I must say they fighted well.
17 Tom never drinks alcoholics.
18 Let's discuss about the problem.
19 It's not beer, but wine.
20 Her sister is twenty-nine years.
21 Her man is Australian.
22 He lets his car washed every week.
23 Her father is very old – she must look for him.
24 The Wednesday is the middle of the week.
25 Ask the policeman what is happened.
26 They eat every time the same thing.
27 "Good evening!" she shouted at me.
28 I went to Madrid for learning Spanish.
29 Jazz is an art of music.
30 "Wouldn't you like to go?" – "Yes, I wouldn't."

1 She has **always** collected photos of pop stars. (199)
2 What **does** "dog" **mean** in German? (194)
3 He likes to **go for** a walk in the evening. (191)
4 My jacket has three **buttons**. (207)
5 She can type, **can't she**? (185)
6 His car is **different from** ours. (210)
7 I haven't got **enough money**. (184)
8 This is a very hard **job**. (201)
9 **Time** flies. (202)
10 What **does it say** on the back of the book? (197)
11 **How** do you know my name? (211)
12 Munich is a nice **city**. (198)
13 I need something **for** headaches. (200)
14 **Sorry I'm** late. (208)
15 The dog ran **after** the cat. (190)
16 Borussia lost, but I must say they **fought** well. (205)
17 Tom never drinks **alcohol**. (209)
18 Let's **discuss** the problem. (188)
19 It's not beer, **it's** wine. (204)
20 Her sister is **twenty-nine**. (79)
21 Her **husband** is Australian. (195)
22 He **has** his car washed every week. (206)
23 Her father is very old – she must look **after** him. (100)
24 **Wednesday** is the middle of the week. (186)
25 Ask the policeman what **has** happened. (196)
26 They **always eat** the same thing. (203)
27 "Good evening!" she shouted **to** me. (187)
28 I went to Madrid **to learn** Spanish. (193)
29 Jazz is **a kind** of music. (189)
30 "Wouldn't you like to go?" – "**No, I wouldn't**." / "**Yes, I would**." (192)

1 She went to the shop for buying bread.
2 "Hey, that's my beer you're drinking!" – "Oh, excuse me!"
3 I bought something against flu.
4 I don't eat many fruits.
5 Look for the cat – it's drinking out of the goldfish bowl!
6 Can you tell me what is happened?
7 What means "cheap" in German?
8 "She's French." – "Where do you know that from?"
9 My baggage was controlled at the airport.
10 Football fans drink too much alcoholics.
11 We can't go for a walk by this weather.
12 They go every time to the same restaurant.
13 The love is something beautiful.
14 I'll speak to her when she will return.
15 Her man is a Borussia fan.
16 London is an interesting town.
17 What stands on the sign over there?
18 He spends hours reading on his desk.

19 "Can't you swim?" – "Yes, I can't."
20 It's not French, but Italian.
21 My father is sixty-one years.
22 His job is other than hers.
23 I make a walk every evening.
24 Let's go for a walk after the lunch.
25 How many buttoms has your coat got?
26 I have ever been interested in the cinema.
27 She lets her windows cleaned every week.
28 You needn't to work tomorrow.
29 That's a difficult work.
30 The two sisters fighted like cat and dog.

1 She went to the shop **to buy** bread. (193)
2 "Hey, that's my beer you're drinking!" – "Oh, **I'm sorry**!" (208)
3 I bought something **for** flu. (200)
4 I don't eat **much fruit**. (216)
5 Look **at** the cat – it's drinking out of the goldfish bowl! (100)
6 Can you tell me what **has** happened? (196)
7 What **does** "cheap" **mean** in German? (194)
8 "She's French." – "**How** do you know that?" (211)
9 My baggage was **checked** at the airport. (212)
10 Football fans drink too much **alcohol**. (209)
11 We can't go for a walk **in** this weather. (213)
12 They **always go** to the same restaurant. (203)
13 **Love** is something beautiful. (202)
14 I'll speak to her when she **returns**. (214)
15 Her **husband** is a Borussia fan. (195)
16 London is an interesting **city**. (198)
17 What **does it say** on the sign over there? (197)
18 He spends hours reading **at** his desk. (215)
19 "Can't you swim?" – "**Yes, I can**." / "**No, I can't**." (192)
20 It's not French, **it's** Italian. (204)
21 My father is **sixty-one**. (79)
22 His job is **different from** hers. (210)
23 I **go for** a walk every evening. (191)
24 Let's go for a walk after **lunch**. (218)
25 How many **buttons** has your coat got? (207)
26 I have **always** been interested in the cinema. (199)
27 She **has** her windows cleaned every week. (206)
28 You **needn't work** tomorrow. (217)
29 That's a difficult **job**. (201)
30 The two sisters **fought** like cat and dog. (205)

1 We'll see them when they will arrive.
2 People under sixteen shouldn't drink alcoholics.
3 I let my car serviced every 10,000 km.
4 You won the first prize! Congratulation!
5 Paris is a beautiful town.
6 We like tennis – it makes fun!
7 Beer isn't so expensive like wine.
8 Have you got anything against a cold?
9 You can't play tennis by this weather.
10 This isn't a very interesting work.
11 "He's the killer!" – "Where do you know that from?"
12 Last year beer cost two mark.
13 He buys every time the same type of car.
14 The airport guard controlled the handbags.
15 We needn't to do overtime today.
16 That wine is other than this one.
17 How can you sit on your desk for so many hours?
18 Can you sew this buttom on my shirt, please?
19 I spent an hour looking after my book.
20 "Now you've broken my pencil!" – "Oh, excuse me!"
21 The two cities fighted each other for many years.
22 I always sleep long on Sundays.
23 Beuys lived for the art.
24 At first I learnt French and then Spanish.
25 Our mother is fifty-five years.
26 She has ever drunk coffee in the morning.
27 My wife bought some fruits in the shop.
28 We need another tin of colour for the bedroom.
29 It's not cold, but very hot.
30 John went to bed after the dinner.

1 We'll see them when they **arrive**. (214)
2 People under sixteen shouldn't drink **alcohol**. (209)
3 I **have** my car serviced every 10,000 km. (206)
4 You won the first prize! **Congratulations**! (219)
5 Paris is a beautiful **city**. (198)
6 We like tennis – **it's fun**! (223)
7 Beer isn't **as** expensive **as** wine. (221)
8 Have you got anything **for** a cold? (200)
9 You can't play tennis **in** this weather. (213)
10 This isn't a very interesting **job**. (201)
11 "He's the killer!" – "**How** do you know that?" (211)
12 Last year beer cost two **marks**. (224)
13 He **always buys** the same type of car. (203)
14 The airport guard **checked** the handbags. (212)
15 We **needn't do** overtime today. (217)
16 That wine is **different from** this one. (210)
17 How can you sit **at** your desk for so many hours? (215)
18 Can you sew this **button** on my shirt, please? (207)
19 I spent an hour looking **for** my book. (100)
20 "Now you've broken my pencil!" – "Oh, **I'm sorry**!" (208)
21 The two cities **fought** each other for many years. (205)
22 I always **have a lie-in** on Sundays. (225)
23 Beuys lived for **art**. (202)
24 **First** I learnt French and then Spanish. (222)
25 Our mother is **fifty-five**. (79)
26 She has **always** drunk coffee in the morning. (199)
27 My wife bought some **fruit** in the shop. (216)
28 We need another tin of **paint** for the bedroom. (220)
29 It's not cold, **it's** very hot. (204)
30 John went to bed **after dinner**. (218)

1 His brother is twenty-two years.
2 He's looking after his money – he lost it here yesterday.
3 I let the flat painted every two years.
4 There is a buttom missing on my shirt.
5 "You're late again, Tom!" – "Excuse me, Mr Smith!"
6 Everybody drinks alcoholics at a party.
7 His hobbies are other than mine.
8 "They're Italians." – "Where do you know that from?"
9 The border guards controlled every car.
10 I'm not going out by that weather!
11 We'll go out when the rain will stop.
12 I've been sitting on my desk all day.
13 What kind of fruits do you like?
14 He needn't to come early tomorrow.
15 My wife left the house after the breakfast.
16 Congratulation on your win!
17 The tin of colour fell off the ladder.
18 London isn't so warm like Seville.
19 At first we had a drink and then we had dinner.
20 I love horse-riding – it makes fun!
21 The wine cost eight mark yesterday.
22 Do you always sleep long on Sundays?
23 I went to the cinema and after then to the pub.
24 Let's meet us at seven.
25 She cut herself in the hand with the scissors.
26 What time did they bring the tennis last night?
27 I remember me on my first day at school.
28 He bought the house before ten years.
29 Where's the photo who I took last week?
30 The film starts at five past eight o'clock.

1 His brother is **twenty-two**. (79)
2 He's looking **for** his money – he lost it here yesterday. (100)
3 I **have** the flat painted every two years. (206)
4 There is a **button** missing on my shirt. (207)
5 "You're late again, Tom!" – "**I'm sorry**, Mr Smith!" (208)
6 Everybody drinks **alcohol** at a party. (209)
7 His hobbies are **different from** mine. (210)
8 "They're Italians." – "**How** do you know that?" (211)
9 The border guards **checked** every car. (212)
10 I'm not going out **in** that weather! (213)
11 We'll go out when the rain **stops**. (214)
12 I've been sitting **at** my desk all day. (215)
13 What kind of **fruit** do you like? (216)
14 He **needn't come** early tomorrow. (217)
15 My wife left the house **after breakfast**. (218)
16 **Congratulations** on your win! (219)
17 The tin of **paint** fell off the ladder. (220)
18 London isn't **as** warm **as** Seville. (221)
19 **First** we had a drink and then we had dinner. (222)
20 I love horse-riding – **it's fun**! (223)
21 The wine cost eight **marks** yesterday. (224)
22 Do you always **have a lie-in** on Sundays? (225)
23 I went to the cinema and after **that** to the pub. (226)
24 **Let's meet** at seven. (227)
25 She cut **her hand** with the scissors. (228)
26 What time did they **show** the tennis last night? (229)
27 I **remember** my first day at school. (230)
28 He bought the house **ten years ago**. (231)
29 Where's the photo **which** I took last week? (232)
30 The film starts at five past **eight**. (233)

1 Mein Vater ist sechzig Jahre alt.
2 Sieh dir den an – er ist total betrunken.
3 Ich lasse jede Woche mein Auto waschen.
4 Der Mantel hat drei Knöpfe.
5 Tut mir leid, daß ich zu spät komme.
6 Kinder sollten keinen Alkohol trinken.
7 Dein Leben ist anders als meins.
8 Woher wissen Sie das?
9 Beim Zoll wird jedes Auto kontrolliert.
10 Bei diesem Wetter gehen wir nicht spazieren!
11 Ich gebe dir das Buch, wenn du wieder da bist.
12 Er sitzt den ganzen Tag an seinem Schreibtisch.
13 Es gibt mehr Obst im Sommer.
14 Sie braucht morgen nicht zu kommen.
15 Nach dem Mittagessen muß ich wieder arbeiten.
16 Du hast gewonnen! Herzlichen Glückwunsch!
17 Ich habe gestern noch eine Dose Farbe gekauft.
18 München ist nicht so groß wie Tokio.
19 Zuerst haben wir gegessen, dann sind wir ins Kino gegangen.
20 Das macht Spaß!
21 Das Buch hat letztes Jahr zwanzig Mark gekostet.
22 Samstags schlafen wir immer lange.
23 Ich bin nach Bonn gefahren, und hinterher nach Köln.
24 Wir treffen uns im Restaurant.
25 Hast du dir in die Hand geschnitten?
26 Bringen sie heute das Spiel live?
27 Ich erinnere mich an unseren ersten Urlaub.
28 Er hat Bremen vor zwei Jahren verlassen.
29 Das ist der Film, den ich letzte Woche gesehen habe.
30 Wir fangen um zehn nach sieben an.

1 My father is sixty. (79)
2 Look at him – he's completely drunk! (100)
3 I have my car washed every week. (206)
4 The coat has got three buttons. (207)
5 Sorry I'm late. (208)
6 Children shouldn't drink alcohol. (209)
7 Your life is different from mine. (210)
8 How do you know that? (211)
9 Every car is checked at the customs. (212)
10 We're not going for a walk in this weather! (213)
11 I'll give you the book when you're here again. (214)
12 He sits at his desk the whole day. (215)
13 There's more fruit in the summer. (216)
14 She needn't come tomorrow. (217)
15 After lunch I must work again. (218)
16 You won! Congratulations! (219)
17 I bought another tin of paint yesterday. (220)
18 Munich isn't as big as Tokio. (221)
19 First we ate, then we went to the cinema. (222)
20 That's fun! (223)
21 The book cost twenty marks last year. (224)
22 We always have a lie-in on Saturdays. (225)
23 I went to Bonn and after that to Cologne. (226)
24 We're meeting in the restaurant. (227)
25 Have you cut your hand? (228)
26 Are they showing the game live today? (229)
27 I remember our first holiday. (230)
28 He left Bremen two years ago. (231)
29 That's the film which I saw last week. (232)
30 We start at ten past seven. (233)

1 My wife likes to sleep long on Sundays.
2 He lets his hair cut every month.
3 The heaven was dark blue.
4 Where is my scissors?
5 We met us at the station.
6 The customs control every tenth car.
7 He cut himself in the foot with an axe.
8 Tennis is wonderful – it makes fun!
9 Didn't they bring any football on ZDF?
10 We'll go when the last guest will leave.
11 I needn't to get up early tomorrow.
12 Sit on the table and eat, children.
13 I started working here before two years.
14 You should eat more fruits.
15 I saw the glasses who were on the table yesterday.
16 I remember me on my first holiday in France.
17 I get home at ten to six o'clock.
18 We went swimming before the breakfast.
19 It's your turn to spend the coffee and cake.
20 You're getting married! Congratulation!
21 She had luck – she found her money again.
22 We have to buy more colour for the living room.
23 Where is your brother born?
24 Bonn isn't so big like Hamburg.
25 We watched the match and after then I drove to the pub.
26 At first we played golf and then we had a drink.
27 I'm interesting in sport.
28 Do you really want to go for a walk by that weather?
29 Excuse me. I have a question to that point.
30 The magazine cost six mark two years ago.

1 My wife likes to **have a lie-in** on Sundays. (225)
2 He **has** his hair cut every month. (206)
3 The **sky** was dark blue. (237)
4 Where **are** my scissors? (50)
5 We **met** at the station. (227)
6 The customs **check** every tenth car. (212)
7 He cut **his foot** with an axe. (228)
8 Tennis is wonderful – **it's fun**! (223)
9 Didn't they **show** any football on ZDF? (229)
10 We'll go when the last guest **leaves**. (214)
11 I **needn't get up** early tomorrow. (217)
12 Sit **at** the table and eat, children. (215)
13 I started working here **two years ago**. (231)
14 You should eat more **fruit**. (216)
15 I saw the glasses **which** were on the table yesterday. (232)
16 I **remember** my first holiday in France. (230)
17 I get home at ten to **six**. (233)
18 We went swimming **before breakfast**. (218)
19 It's your turn to **buy** the coffee and cake. (234)
20 You're getting married! **Congratulations**! (219)
21 She **was lucky** – she found her money again. (235)
22 We have to buy more **paint** for the living room. (220)
23 Where **was** your brother born? (236)
24 Bonn isn't **as** big **as** Hamburg. (221)
25 We watched the match and after **that** I drove to the pub. (226)
26 **First** we played golf and then we had a drink. (222)
27 I'm **interested** in sport. (238)
28 Do you really want to go for a walk **in** that weather? (213)
29 Excuse me, I have a question **on** that point. (239)
30 The magazine cost six **marks** two years ago. (224)

1 What can you see in the heaven at night?
2 Where can we meet us?
3 They went to the cinema after the dinner.
4 He's interesting in jazz.
5 I've cut myself in the finger!
6 I can't see anything – my glasses is dirty.
7 May I ask you a question to your report?
8 They wanted to bring the match live.
9 Your first child! Congratulation!
10 You have to cook the water first.
11 I remember me on the first test at school.
12 Do we need more colour to finish the job?
13 You can buy at Horten books.
14 They left Bremen before three years.
15 Mont Blanc isn't so high like Everest.
16 Ask the waiter for the card.
17 That's the book who I was looking for.
18 At first we finished the work and then we went for a walk.
19 I'll become thirty-three tomorrow.
20 The programme starts at ten past seven o'clock.
21 I like going to the disco – it makes fun!
22 It's nice to be under friends again.
23 In twenty years Smith has never spent a round of drinks.
24 The trip cost eighty dollar in 1970.
25 What time do you go up in the morning!
26 He had luck – he won the first prize twice.
27 I never have a chance to sleep long.
28 Is your son good in German?
29 I am born in Germany.
30 She went to the shops and after then to the station.

1 What can you see in the **sky** at night? (237)

2 Where can we **meet**? (227)

3 They went to the cinema **after dinner**. (218)

4 He's **interested** in jazz. (238)

5 I've cut **my finger**! (228)

6 I can't see anything – my glasses **are** dirty. (50)

7 May I ask you a question **on** your report? (239)

8 They wanted to **show** the match live. (229)

9 Your first child! **Congratulations**! (219)

10 You have to **boil** the water first. (95)

11 I **remember** the first test at school. (230)

12 Do we need more **paint** to finish the job? (220)

13 You can buy **books at Horten**. (241)

14 They left Bremen **three years ago**. (231)

15 Mont Blanc isn't **as** high **as** Everest. (221)

16 Ask the waiter for the **menu**. (242)

17 That's the book **which** I was looking for. (232)

18 **First** we finished the work and then we went for a walk. (222)

19 I'll **be** thirty-three tomorrow. (243)

20 The programme starts at ten past **seven**. (233)

21 I like going going to the disco – **it's fun**! (223)

22 It's nice to be **among** friends again. (244)

23 In twenty years Smith has never **bought** a round of drinks. (234)

24 The trip cost eighty **dollars** in 1970. (224)

25 What time do you **get up** in the morning! (245)

26 He **was lucky** – he won the first prize twice. (235)

27 I never have a chance to **have a lie-in**. (225)

28 Is your son good **at** German? (246)

29 I **was** born in Germany. (236)

30 She went to the shops and after **that** to the station. (226)

1 John's good in French, but he's even better in maths.
2 Are you interesting in football?
3 She arrived here before two hours.
4 We don't make that difference between the two in our language.
5 England won the World Cup for many years.
6 Do you have any questions to this problem?
7 Show me the dress who you bought yesterday.
8 This trousers is too big for me.
9 Should we cook the water before we drink it?
10 I leave the house at five to five o'clock.
11 He played tennis and after then he went home.
12 The motor's at the back in the VW Beetle.
13 You can see at the cinema films.
14 Come on – I'll spend you a beer.
15 What time are we going to meet us?
16 She stood besides him watching the match.
17 This restaurant has some excellent dishes on the card.
18 I had luck – I married the right woman.
19 Be careful – don't cut yourself in the finger!
20 He were here yesterday.
21 My brother will become forty next year.
22 What year are you born in?
23 They never bring squash live on television.
24 Whisky is double as expensive as wine.
25 It's easier to relax under friends.
26 The heaven is clear – look at the stars!
27 I remember me on my first trip to the zoo.
28 I have a date with my dentist tomorrow.
29 What time did you go up yesterday?
30 I like chess – it makes fun!

1 John's good **at** French, but he's even better **at** maths. (246)
2 Are you **interested** in football? (238)
3 She arrived here **two hours ago**. (231)
4 We don't **distinguish** between the two in our language. (248)
5 England won the World Cup **many years ago**. (247)
6 Do you have any questions **about** this problem? (239)
7 Show me the dress **which** you bought yesterday. (232)
8 **These** trousers **are** too big for me. (50)
9 Should we **boil** the water before we drink it? (95)
10 I leave the house at five to **five**. (233)
11 He played tennis and after **that** he went home. (226)
12 The **engine**'s at the back in the VW Beetle. (249)
13 You can see **films at the cinema**. (241)
14 Come on – I'll **buy** you a beer. (234)
15 What time are we going to **meet**? (227)
16 She stood **beside** him watching the match. (252)
17 This restaurant has some excellent dishes on the **menu**. (242)
18 I **was lucky** – I married the right woman. (235)
19 Be careful – don't cut **your finger**! (228)
20 He **was** here yesterday. (253)
21 My brother will **be** forty next year. (243)
22 What year **were** you born in? (236)
23 They never **show** squash live on television. (229)
24 Whisky is **twice** as expensive as wine. (250)
25 It's easier to relax **among** friends. (244)
26 The **sky** is clear – look at the stars! (237)
27 I **remember** my first trip to the zoo. (230)
28 I have **an appointment** with my dentist tomorrow. (251)
29 What time did you **get up** yesterday? (245)
30 I like chess – **it's fun**! (223)

1 She's tired, therefore she's going to bed.
2 It costs double as much in England.
3 It's great to be under friends again.
4 Aren't you interesting in politics?
5 The film started before ten minutes.
6 I am used to work on my own.
7 My wife has a date with the lawyer tomorrow.
8 I always go up late on Sundays.
9 Do you want to ask a question to this problem?
10 Is this your scissors?
11 His wife drove to town with the bus.
12 Come here, and sit besides me.
13 I was never good in history at school.
14 You can't cook water on that fire!
15 Let's go to the pub – I'll spend you a drink.
16 I was already in England.
17 Was you here yesterday?
18 I got married for ten years.
19 You can see in an art gallery pictures.
20 I had luck at poker – I won fifty marks.
21 Her coat protected her against the cold.
22 We make sport twice a week.
23 Don't you make that difference between the two in French?
24 (In a restaurant) I'm hungry – may I have the card, please?
25 She is born here fifty years ago.
26 We needn't any money.
27 He always has a big lunch in the evening.
28 Phone for a taxi – the motor won't start.
29 She'll become twenty-one in May.
30 The heaven was pink yesterday evening.

1 She's tired, **so** she's going to bed. (256)

2 It costs **twice** as much in England. (250)

3 It's great to be **among** friends again. (244)

4 Aren't you **interested** in politics? (238)

5 The film started **ten minutes ago**. (231)

6 I am used to **working** on my own. (257)

7 My wife has **an appointment** with the lawyer tomorrow. (251)

8 I always **get up** late on Sundays. (245)

9 Do you want to ask a question **about** this problem? (239)

10 **Are these** your scissors? (50)

11 His wife **went** to town **by** bus. (258)

12 Come here, and sit **beside** me. (252)

13 I was never good **at** history at school. (246)

14 You can't **boil** water on that fire! (95)

15 Let's go to the pub – I'll **buy** you a drink. (234)

16 **I've already been to** England. (259)

17 **Were** you here yesterday? (253)

18 I got married **ten years ago**. (247)

19 You can see **pictures in an art gallery**. (241)

20 I **was lucky** at poker – I won fifty marks. (235)

21 Her coat protected her **from** the cold. (260)

22 We **do** sport twice a week. (254)

23 Don't you **distinguish** between the two in French? (248)

24 (In a restaurant) I'm hungry – may I have the **menu**, please? (242)

25 She **was** born here fifty years ago. (236)

26 We **don't need** any money. (261)

27 He always has a big **dinner** in the evening. (255)

28 Phone for a taxi – the **engine** won't start. (249)

29 She'll **be** twenty-one in May. (243)

30 The **sky** was pink yesterday evening. (237)

1 Ich habe sie vor zehn Minuten angerufen.
2 Meine Brille ist kaputt.
3 Kommt! Ich spendiere eine Runde Bier!
4 Ich hatte Glück – ich habe alles gewonnen.
5 Wo ist sie geboren?
6 Was sieht man abends am Himmel?
7 Er interessiert sich für Musik.
8 Entschuldigung – eine Frage zum letzten Punkt.
9 Das Wasser kocht!
10 Du kannst bei Koch Filme kaufen.
11 Herr Ober, können Sie mir bitte die Karte bringen?
12 Morgen werde ich einundzwanzig.
13 Wir sind hier unter Freunden.
14 Wir müssen morgen um fünf aufstehen.
15 In der Schule war ich gut in Sprachen.
16 Vor zehn Jahren haben wir in Spanien eine Villa gebaut.
17 Ich brauche kein Geld.
18 Wo ist der Motor beim VW Käfer?
19 Das kostet doppelt soviel in England.
20 Meine Frau hat morgen einen Termin beim Friseur.
21 Außer Wasser trinken wir gar nichts.
22 Er war gestern in Aachen.
23 Jedes Kind sollte Sport treiben.
24 Das Mittagessen in der Kantine ist sehr gut.
25 Ich bin müde, deshalb gehe ich ins Bett.
26 Sie ist es nicht gewohnt, links zu fahren.
27 Er ist mit dem Bus nach Düsseldorf gefahren.
28 Waren Sie schon einmal in Griechenland?
29 Dieser dünne Mantel wird dich nicht vor der Kälte schützen.
30 Machen die Deutschen keinen Unterschied zwischen den beiden?

1 I phoned her ten minutes ago. (231)
2 My glasses are broken. (50)
3 Come on! I'll buy a round of beer! (234)
4 I was lucky – I won everything. (235)
5 Where was she born? (236)
6 What can you see in the sky in the evening? (237)
7 He's interested in music. (238)
8 Excuse me – a question about the last point. (239)
9 The water is boiling! (95)
10 You can buy films at Koch's. (241)
11 Waiter, can you bring me the menu, please? (242)
12 I'll be twenty-one tomorrow. (243)
13 We are among friends here. (244)
14 We must get up at five tomorrow. (245)
15 I was good at languages at school. (246)
16 We built a villa in Spain ten years ago. (247)
17 I don't need any money. (261)
18 Where's the engine in a VW Beetle? (249)
19 That costs twice as much in England. (250)
20 My wife has an appointment at the hairdresser's tomorrow. (251)
21 Besides water we don't drink anything at all. (252)
22 He was in Aachen yesterday. (253)
23 Every child should do sport. (254)
24 Lunch in the canteen is very good. (255)
25 I'm tired, so I'm going to bed. (256)
26 She isn't used to driving on the left. (257)
27 He went to Düsseldorf by bus. (258)
28 Have you ever been to Greece? (259)
29 That thin coat won't protect you from the cold. (260)
30 Don't the Germans distinguish between the two? (248)

1 The programme begins at nineteen o'clock.
2 We can drive to Bonn with the train.
3 She were at school yesterday.
4 You have to make a difference between the two!
5 He will become eighteen in June.
6 If he will make money, he must work harder.
7 London is the largest city of England.
8 We help one another – that's normal under colleagues.
9 Were you already in Spain?
10 Did you make any sport as a child?
11 I'm hungry, therefore I'm making myself a sandwich.
12 I need a taxi – I can't start the motor.
13 My trousers is light blue.
14 Can you drive a motor-bike?
15 My umbrella protected me against the rain.
16 Did you have a good lunch last night?
17 Hotels are double as expensive in my country.
18 I have no other hobbies beside tennis and golf.
19 Where can I cook water?
20 Ten marks are a lot of money for a coffee.
21 I needn't any more books.
22 Were you good in languages at school?
23 You can take with a camera photos.
24 He made the work well.
25 I don't like her kind of living.
26 She isn't used to speak French all day.
27 I must go up early during the week.
28 He started working here for six years.
29 (In a restaurant) Can I see the card, please?
30 My husband has a date with his doctor on Friday.

1 The programme begins at **seven** o'clock (in the evening). (263)
2 We can **go** to Bonn **by** train. (258)
3 She **was** at school yesterday. (253)
4 You have to **distinguish** between the two! (248)
5 He will **be** eighteen in June. (243)
6 If he **wants to** make money, he must work harder. (90)
7 London is the largest city **in** England. (264)
8 We help one another – that's normal **among** colleagues. (244)
9 **Have you ever been to** Spain? (259)
10 Did you **do** any sport as a child? (254)
11 I'm hungry, **so** I'm making myself a sandwich. (256)
12 I need a taxi – I can't start the **engine**. (249)
13 My trousers **are** light blue. (50)
14 Can you **ride** a motor-bike? (265)
15 My umbrella protected me **from** the rain. (260)
16 Did you have a good **dinner** last night? (255)
17 Hotels are **twice** as expensive in my country. (250)
18 I have no other hobbies **besides** tennis and golf. (252)
19 Where can I **boil** water? (95)
20 Ten marks **is** a lot of money for a coffee. (266)
21 I **don't need** any more books. (261)
22 Were you good **at** languages at school? (246)
23 You can take photos **with a camera**. (241)
24 He **did** the work well. (267)
25 I don't like her **way** of living. (262)
26 She isn't used to **speaking** French all day. (257)
27 I must **get up** early during the week. (245)
28 He started working here **six years ago**. (247)
29 (In a restaurant) Can I see the **menu**, please? (242)
30 My husband has **an appointment** with his doctor on Friday. (251)

1 How's about a drink?
2 He's the famoust Italian painter.
3 Can't we drive with the tram?
4 Are you used to drive on the left now?
5 They was very nice.
6 Is the motor at the front or back of a VW?
7 If he will go, he can go!
8 The woman wore a shopping-bag in her hand.
9 Twenty years in prison are a long time.
10 I don't understand his kind of explaining things.
11 They needn't any more free time.
12 We made a lot of sport at school.
13 The sofa is double as heavy as the chair.
14 The scissors is on the table.
15 There is a new American TV serie on television tonight.
16 Did they make the work correctly?
17 The film starts at twenty o'clock.
18 Was your son already in America?
19 After a big dinner I can't work in the afternoon.
20 I have a date with my bank manager at four.
21 She won the lottery for five years.
22 That's what he told to me.
23 What's your chief like?
24 America is the richest country of the world.
25 The beach umbrella protected us against the heat.
26 He's thirsty, therefore he's drinking a glass of water.
27 Have you lived in other countries beside Germany?
28 I've tried to make a difference between the two.
29 My brother can drive a motor-bike.
30 The film plays in America.

1 **How** about a drink? (268)
2 He's the **most famous** Italian painter. (274)
3 Can't we **go by** tram? (258)
4 Are you used to **driving** on the left now? (257)
5 They **were** very nice. (253)
6 Is the **engine** at the front or back of a VW? (249)
7 If he **wants to** go, he can go! (90)
8 The woman **carried** a shopping-bag in her hand. (271)
9 Twenty years in prison **is** a long time. (266)
10 I don't understand his **way** of explaining things. (262)
11 They **don't need** any more free time. (261)
12 We **did** a lot of sport at school. (254)
13 The sofa is **twice** as heavy as the chair. (250)
14 The scissors **are** on the table. (50)
15 There is a new American TV **series** on television tonight. (272)
16 Did they **do** the work correctly? (267)
17 The film starts at **eight** o'clock (in the evening). (263)
18 **Has** your son **ever been to** America? (259)
19 After a big **lunch** I can't work in the afternoon. (255)
20 I have **an appointment** with my bank manager at four. (251)
21 She won the lottery **five years ago**. (247)
22 That's what he **told me**. (273)
23 What's your **boss** like? (270)
24 America is the richest country **in** the world. (264)
25 The beach umbrella protected us **from** the heat. (260)
26 He's thirsty, **so** he's drinking a glass of water. (256)
27 Have you lived in other countries **besides** Germany? (252)
28 I've tried to **distinguish** between the two. (248)
29 My brother can **ride** a motor-bike. (265)
30 The film **is set** in America. (269)

1 What's about a cup of tea?
2 Who's England's famoust writer?
3 We needn't any more beer for the party.
4 Twenty dollars are too much for the book.
5 His kind of living isn't very healthy.
6 Why don't you drive with the taxi?
7 "How are you?" – "Thank you, fine."
8 I always wear an umbrella with me.
9 Does she make her work well?
10 I finish work at eighteen o'clock.
11 Were they already in Italy?
12 My chief is a nice person.
13 The trousers has a brown belt.
14 Are that my photos?
15 He's got all his money on the bank.
16 What time is the serie on television?
17 The story plays in Italy.
18 I'm not used to get up so early.
19 How much sport do you make?

20 They're tired, therefore they're going home.
21 If they will work in Paris, they must learn French.
22 (Tel.) "Who's speaking, please?" – "Mr Schmidt is speaking."
23 Yesterday I went at home early.
24 You have more money as your sister.
25 What did he tell to you?
26 Heidelberg is the prettiest town of Germany.
27 The special clothing protected him against the cold.
28 What for a drink is it?
29 I could drive a bike at five.
30 After a big dinner he needs a siesta.

1 **What** about a cup of tea? (268)
2 Who's England's **most famous** writer? (274)
3 We **don't need** any more beer for the party. (261)
4 Twenty dollars **is** too much for the book. (266)
5 His **way** of living isn't very healthy. (262)
6 Why don't you **go by** taxi? (258)
7 "How are you?" – "**Fine, thank you**." (280)
8 I always **carry** an umbrella with me. (271)
9 Does she **do** her work well? (267)
10 I finish work at **six** o'clock (in the evening). (263)
11 **Have** they **ever been to** Italy? (259)
12 My **boss** is a nice person. (270)
13 The trousers **have** a brown belt. (50)
14 Are **those** my photos? (281)
15 He's got all his money **in** the bank. (276)
16 What time is the **series** on television? (272)
17 The story **is set** in Italy. (269)
18 I'm not used to **getting up** so early. (257)
19 How much sport do you **do**? (254)
20 They're tired, **so** they're going home. (256)
21 If they **want to** work in Paris, they must learn French. (90)
22 (Tel.) "Who's speaking, please?" – "**Schmidt speaking**." (279)
23 Yesterday I **went home** early. (277)
24 You have more money **than** your sister. (275)
25 What did he **tell you**? (273)
26 Heidelberg is the prettiest town **in** Germany. (264)
27 The special clothing protected him **from** the cold. (260)
28 **What kind of** drink is it? (278)
29 I could **ride** a bike at five. (265)
30 After a big **lunch** he needs a siesta. (255)

1 How's about a coffee?
2 I arrive eight o'clock.
3 (Tel.) "Who's speaking, please?" – "Mr Braun is speaking."
4 He has more free time as John.
5 What's your favourite TV serie?
6 The film played in Russia.
7 We leave the factory at twenty-two o'clock.
8 Six years at university are a long time.
9 If you will have a job here, you must work harder.
10 This word isn't existing in German.
11 They asked me who was my partner.
12 What for a game is it?
13 My money is on the bank.
14 She wore the bag in her left hand.
15 Can you make the work tomorrow?
16 How's your chief?
17 Berlin is the largest city of Germany.
18 I can't see – where is my glasses?
19 Which time is it?
20 He's the man he left early.
21 When did she come at home last night?
22 "How are you?" – "Thank you."
23 She is the famoust politician in the world.
24 I don't know what to tell to her.
25 This are tropical plants.
26 Most children can drive a bike.
27 Her kind of speaking is very monotonous.
28 The pub is in the near of my house.
29 The fly to New York was good.
30 Can I have fire, please?

1 **How** about a coffee? (268)
2 I arrive **at** eight o'clock. (288)
3 (Tel.) "Who's speaking, please?" – "**Braun speaking**." (279)
4 He has more free time **than** John. (275)
5 What's your favourite TV **series**? (272)
6 The film **was set** in Russia. (269)
7 We leave the factory at **ten** o'clock (in the evening). (263)
8 Six years at university **is** a long time. (266)
9 If you **want to** have a job here, you must work harder. (90)
10 This word **doesn't exist** in German. (287)
11 They asked me who my partner **was**. (283)
12 **What kind of** game is it? (278)
13 My money is **in** the bank. (276)
14 She **carried** the bag in her left hand. (271)
15 Can you **do** the work tomorrow? (267)
16 How's your **boss**? (270)
17 Berlin is the largest city **in** Germany. (264)
18 I can't see – where **are** my glasses? (50)
19 **What** time is it? (289)
20 He's the man **who** left early. (284)
21 When did she **come home** last night? (277)
22 "How are you?" – "**Fine, thank you**." (280)
23 She is the **most famous** politician in the world. (274)
24 I don't know what to **tell her**. (273)
25 **These** are tropical plants. (281)
26 Most children can **ride** a bike. (265)
27 Her **way** of speaking is very monotonous. (262)
28 The pub is **near** my house. (282)
29 The **flight** to New York was good. (285)
30 Can I have **a light**, please? (286)

1 Wenn sie gewinnen will, muß sie mehr trainieren.
2 Meine Hose ist schmutzig.
3 Ich mag die Art nicht, wie er redet.
4 Die Läden machen um achtzehn Uhr zu.
5 Tokio ist die größte Stadt Japans.
6 Kann deine Schwester Motorrad fahren?
7 Zehn Dollar sind zuviel!
8 Ich muß sagen, Sie machen Ihre Arbeit gut.
9 Wie wär's mit einem Eis?
10 Der Film spielt in Berlin.
11 Der Chef ist ein Fachmann.
12 Er trug das Kind auf dem Rücken.
13 Das ist die neue englische TV-Serie.
14 Das habe ich Ihnen gesagt.
15 Er war der berühmteste Tenor der Welt.
16 Sie hat mehr Zeit als Hans.
17 Ich habe mein ganzes Geld auf der Bank.
18 Wann bist du gestern nach Hause gekommen?
19 Was für eine Sprache ist das?
20 (Tel.) „Wen darf ich melden?" – „Berger am Apparat."
21 „Wie geht's?" – „Danke, und selbst?"
22 Sind das deine Freunde?
23 Das Kino ist in der Nähe vom Supermarkt.
24 Er fragte mich, wie alt ich sei.
25 Er ist der Mann, der hier wohnt.
26 Wie war dein Flug?
27 Können Sie mir bitte Feuer geben?
28 Das Hotel existiert nicht mehr.
29 Wir fangen um sieben Uhr an.
30 Wie spät ist es?

1 If she wants to win, she must practise more. (90)
2 My trousers are dirty. (50)
3 I don't like his way of speaking. (262)
4 The shops close at six (in the evening). (263)
5 Tokio is the biggest city in Japan. (264)
6 Can your sister ride a motor bike? (265)
7 Ten dollars is too much! (266)
8 I must say, you do your work well. (267)
9 What about an ice-cream? (268)
10 The film is set in Berlin. (269)
11 The boss is an expert. (270)
12 He carried the child on his back. (271)
13 That's the new English TV series. (272)
14 I told you that. (273)
15 He was the most famous tenor in the world. (274)
16 She's got more time than Hans. (275)
17 I've got all my money in the bank. (276)
18 When did you get home yesterday? (277)
19 What kind of language is that? (278)
20 (Tel.) "Who shall I say is calling?" – "Berger speaking." (279)
21 "How are you?" – "Fine, thanks, and you?" (280)
22 Are those your friends? (281)
23 The cinema is near the supermarket. (282)
24 He asked me how old I was. (283)
25 He's the man who lives here. (284)
26 How was your flight? (285)
27 Can you give me a light, please? (286)
28 The hotel doesn't exist any more. (287)
29 We start at seven o'clock. (288)
30 What time is it? (289)

1 Very interesting! I'll make a notice of that.
2 He has been here since two weeks.
3 Is the word existing in English?
4 She's the girl she studies Spanish.
5 Are this your glasses?
6 What for a beer do you prefer?
7 He earns more as his wife.
8 He was wearing the umbrella in his left hand.
9 The story played in France.
10 If she will be a secretary, she must learn to type.
11 Please? What did you say?
12 "Give me that book, please." – "Please."
13 They start seven o'clock.
14 How was your fly to Rio?
15 The shop is in the near of the station.
16 (Tel.) "Who shall I say is calling?" – "Mr Mueller is calling."
17 "Where is your money?" – "On the bank."
18 What are you going to tell to them?
19 I don't like my chief.
20 That's a good advice.
21 I hear the car radio on the way to work.
22 "What time is it?" – "Seven past two."
23 Which time do you start?
24 Can you give me fire, please?
25 She asked him where was his car.
26 "How's your wife?" – "Thank you."
27 They always come at home late.
28 He was Germany's famoust musician.
29 Oh, no, not another American TV serie!
30 What's about going to the cinema?

1 Very interesting! I'll make a **note** of that. (295)
2 He has been here **for** two weeks. (290)
3 **Does** the word **exist** in English? (287)
4 She's the girl **who** studies Spanish. (284)
5 Are **these** your glasses? (281)
6 What **kind of** beer do you prefer? (278)
7 He earns more **than** his wife. (275)
8 He was **carrying** the umbrella in his left hand. (271)
9 The story **was set** in France. (269)
10 If she **wants to** be a secretary, she must learn to type. (90)
11 **Sorry**? What did you say? (294)
12 "Give me that book, please." – "**Here you are**." (291)
13 They start **at** seven o'clock. (288)
14 How was your **flight** to Rio? (285)
15 The shop is **near** the station. (282)
16 (Tel.) "Who shall I say is calling?" – "**My name is Mueller**." (279)
17 "Where is your money?" – "**In** the bank." (276)
18 What are you going to **tell them**? (273)
19 I don't like my **boss**. (270)
20 That's **good advice**. (117)
21 I **listen to** the car radio on the way to work. (293)
22 "What time is it?" – "Seven **minutes** past two." (292)
23 **What** time do you start? (289)
24 Can you give me **a light**, please? (286)
25 She asked him where his car **was**. (283)
26 "How's your wife?" – "**Fine, thank you**." (280)
27 They always **come home** late. (277)
28 He was Germany's **most famous** musician. (274)
29 Oh, no, not another American TV **series**! (272)
30 **What** about going to the cinema? (268)

1 They travel more as their neighbours.
2 What for a holiday do you like most?
3 That are friends of mine.
4 There's the boy he plays football.
5 "Give me that bottle, please." – "Please."
6 She has been working here since three years.
7 "Where's John?" – "He's hearing the news."
8 My office is in the second floor.
9 Today morning I was in Bonn.
10 I can't go on living so!
11 If you will be a singer, you should take singing lessons.
12 The firm has very strong rules.
13 (Tel.) "Who shall I say is calling?" – "Mr Fischer is calling."
14 We live in the near of the cinema.
15 Did you have a good fly to Paris?
16 Which time did they arrive?
17 Two versions of the book are existing.
18 Please? I didn't hear what you said.
19 "How's your husband?" – "Thank you, fine."
20 Where is the mother company?
21 You should have your money on the bank.
22 A good bed is a necessary furniture.
23 We went at home at five o'clock.
24 I always change Tuesday and Thursday.
25 I wanted to know how old was he.
26 Have you got fire, please?
27 He left six o'clock.
28 The film started at ten minutes past eight.
29 Really? I must make a notice of that.
30 It has been a strong winter.

1 They travel more **than** their neighbours. (275)
2 What **kind of** holiday do you like most? (278)
3 **Those** are friends of mine. (281)
4 There's the boy **who** plays football. (284)
5 "Give me that bottle, please." – "**Here you are**." (291)
6 She has been working here **for** three years. (290)
7 "Where's John?" – "He's **listening to** the news." (293)
8 My office is **on** the second floor. (296)
9 **This** morning I was in Bonn. (299)
10 I can't go on living **like this**! (298)
11 If you **want to** be a singer, you should take singing lessons. (90)
12 The firm has very **strict** rules. (302)
13 (Tel.) "Who shall I say is calling?" – "**Fischer here**." (279)
14 We live **near** the cinema. (282)
15 Did you have a good **flight** to Paris? (285)
16 **What** time did they arrive? (289)
17 Two versions of the book **exist**. (287)
18 **Pardon**? I didn't hear what you said. (294)
19 "How's your husband?" – "**Fine, thank you**." (280)
20 Where is the **parent** company? (300)
21 You should have your money **in** the bank. (276)
22 A good bed is a necessary **piece of furniture**. (117)
23 We **went home** at five o'clock. (277)
24 I always **mix up** Tuesday and Thursday. (297)
25 I wanted to know how old he **was**. (283)
26 Have you got **a light**, please? (286)
27 He left **at** six o'clock. (288)
28 The film started at **ten past** eight. (292)
29 Really? I must make a **note** of that. (295)
30 It has been a **hard** winter. (301)

1 I would go there yesterday.
2 "When shall we start?" – "It's equal."
3 The mother company is in New York.
4 We start at the first of May.
5 Our teacher is very strong!
6 We live in the third floor.
7 They always come five o'clock.
8 Do you have fire, please?
9 Which time are you leaving?
10 He works in the near of Horten.
11 He speaks very well French.
12 You needn't explain – it's clearly.
13 Is that true? I must make a notice of that.
14 Where were you today morning?

15 "What time is it?" – "Six to ten."
16 They have been working in Hamburg since five years.
17 If you will be a millionaire, you should work harder.
18 Please? I didn't hear that.
19 Change your clothes! You can't go out so!
20 How many versions of the film are existing?
21 The fly to Madrid was delayed.
22 He asked me where was John.
23 The doctor gave me a good advice.
24 Susan, you must concentrate yourself more!
25 I'll see you at Friday.
26 Here's the man he works here.
27 I've never known such a strong winter!
28 He always changes a.m. and p.m.
29 "Give me that letter, please." – "Please."
30 "Where's Pauline?" – "She's hearing music in her room."

1 I **wanted to** go there yesterday. (307)
2 "When shall we start?" – "**It doesn't matter**." (309)
3 The **parent** company is in New York. (300)
4 We start **on** the first of May. (304)
5 Our teacher is very **strict**! (302)
6 We live **on** the third floor. (296)
7 They always come **at** five o'clock. (288)
8 Do you have **a light**, please? (286)
9 **What** time are you leaving? (289)
10 He works **near** Horten. (282)
11 He speaks French **very well**. (308)
12 You needn't explain – it's **clear**. (305)
13 Is that true? I must make a **note** of that. (295)
14 Where were you **this** morning? (299)
15 "What time is it?" – "Six **minutes** to ten." (292)
16 They have been working in Hamburg **for** five years. (290)
17 If you **want to** be a millionaire, you should work harder. (90)
18 **Sorry?** I didn't hear that. (294)
19 Change your clothes! You can't go out **like that**! (298)
20 How many versions of the film **exist?** (287)
21 The **flight** to Madrid was delayed. (285)
22 He asked me where John **was**. (283)
23 The doctor gave me **some** good advice. (117)
24 Susan, you must **concentrate** more! (303)
25 I'll see you **on** Friday. (306)
26 Here's the man **who** works here. (284)
27 I've never known such a **hard** winter! (301)
28 He always **confuses** a.m. and p.m. (297)
29 "Give me that letter, please." – "**Here you are**." (291)
30 "Where's Pauline?" – "She's **listening to** music in her room." (293)

1 Be quiet! I'm hearing the radio.
2 "Where shall we go?" – "It's equal."
3 "Here's your paper." – "Do it on my desk, please."
4 I have been living here since six years.
5 The shop opens at the second of June.
6 British schools have very strong rules.
7 Where is the daughter company?
8 Wash your hands! You can't eat so!
9 Let's start at Monday.
10 Please? Could you repeat that?
11 Let's go at twenty minutes to five.
12 We have tennis training once in the week.
13 If you will have more money, you should work overtime.
14 He lives in the Canal Street.
15 This is a heavy job!
16 They have a flat at the fourth floor.
17 Go slowly! You must be carefully!
18 She would play tennis yesterday.
19 Sorry, I wasn't concentrating myself.
20 The last strong winter was in 1962.
21 The traffic was terrible today morning.
22 Hans often changes sky and heaven.
23 That's fascinating! I'll make a notice of that.
24 Would you please be so kind to help me?
25 "Give me that glass, please." – "Please."
26 Yesterday we had a good weather.
27 She phones with Christine once a month.
28 I made a very bad experience in Spain.
29 His hairs are getting grey.
30 She speaks very well Spanish.

1 Be quiet! I'm **listening to** the radio. (293)
2 "Where shall we go?" – "**It doesn't matter**." (309)
3 "Here's your paper." – "**Put** it on my desk, please." (312)
4 I have been living here **for** six years. (290)
5 The shop opens **on** the second of June. (304)
6 British schools have very **strict** rules. (302)
7 Where is the **subsidiary**? (300)
8 Wash your hands! You can't eat **like that**! (298)
9 Let's start **on** Monday. (306)
10 **Pardon?** Could you repeat that? (294)
11 Let's go at **twenty to** five. (292)
12 We have tennis training **once a week**. (310)
13 If you **want to** have more money, you should work overtime. (90)
14 He lives in **Canal Street**. (316)
15 This is a **hard** job! (313)
16 They have a flat **on** the fourth floor. (296)
17 Go slowly! You must be **careful**! (305)
18 She **wanted to** play tennis yesterday. (307)
19 Sorry, I wasn't **concentrating**. (303)
20 The last **bad** winter was in 1962. (301)
21 The traffic was terrible **this** morning. (299)
22 Hans often **confuses** sky and heaven. (297)
23 That's fascinating! I'll make a **note** of that. (295)
24 Would you please be so kind **as** to help me? (315)
25 "Give me that glass, please." – "**Here you are**." (291)
26 Yesterday we had **good weather**. (117)
27 She **phones** Christine once a month. (6)
28 I **had** a very bad experience in Spain. (314)
29 His **hair is** getting grey. (311)
30 She speaks very **good** Spanish. (308)

1 Wenn wir ein neues Auto kaufen wollen, müssen wir mehr Geld sparen.

2 Das ist ein guter Ratschlag.

3 Wir haben seit zwei Wochen einen Hund.

4 „Geben Sie mir bitte den Brief." – „Bitte sehr."

5 „Wie spät ist es?" – „Vier nach sieben."

6 Ich höre jeden Morgen Nachrichten.

7 Bitte? Was haben Sie gesagt?

8 Tatsächlich? Ich mache mir schnell eine Notiz davon.

9 Sie wohnt in der dritten Etage.

10 Wie kann man Gin und Wodka verwechseln?

11 So kann ich nicht weitermachen!

12 Heute morgen war ich im Büro.

13 Die Muttergesellschaft ist in London.

14 Das war ein strenger Winter.

15 Die Lehrer hier sind sehr streng.

16 Nach zwei Glas Wein kann ich mich nicht mehr konzentrieren.

17 Am ersten Mai arbeiten wir nicht.

18 Wir müssen vorsichtig sein.

19 Sie war Freitag hier.

20 Er wollte gestern nach Karlsruhe fahren.

21 Sie spricht sehr gut Englisch.

22 „Wann fahren wir?" – „Das ist egal!"

23 Wir sind einmal die Woche in Bremen.

24 Meine Haare werden grau.

25 „Hier ist dein Glas." – „Tu's bitte auf den Tisch."

26 Es ist schwer, die Arbeit alleine zu machen.

27 In London habe ich nur einmal eine schlechte Erfahrung gemacht.

28 Würden Sie bitte so nett sein, den Brief zu übersetzen?

29 Die King Street ist sehr schön.

30 Wie wär's mit einem Bier?

1 If we want to buy a new car, we must save more money. (90)

2 That's good advice. (117)

3 We have had a dog for two weeks. (290)

4 "Give me the letter, please." – "Here you are." (291)

5 "What time is it?" – "Four minutes past seven." (292)

6 I listen to the news every morning. (293)

7 Sorry? What did you say? (294)

8 Really? I'll make a quick note of that. (295)

9 She lives on the third floor. (296)

10 How can you confuse gin and vodka? (297)

11 I can't go on like this! (298)

12 I was in the office this morning. (299)

13 The parent company is in London. (300)

14 That was a hard winter. (301)

15 The teachers here are very strict. (302)

16 I can't concentrate after two glasses of wine. (303)

17 We don't work on the first of May. (304)

18 We must be careful. (305)

19 She was here on Friday. (306)

20 He wanted to go to Karlsruhe yesterday. (307)

21 She speaks English very well. (308)

22 "When are we going?" – "It doesn't matter!" (309)

23 We are in Bremen once a week. (310)

24 My hair is getting grey. (311)

25 "Here's your glass." – "Put it on the table, please." (312)

26 It's hard to do the work alone. (313)

27 I've only once had a bad experience in London. (314)

28 Would you please be so kind as to translate the letter? (315)

29 King Street is very beautiful. (316)

30 What about a beer? (268)

1 You can see him in television tomorrow.
2 We drove to Munich over Frankfurt.
3 The boss always leave at five o'clock.
4 The soldier's hairs were too long.
5 That's a very light problem.
6 Who said that is an idiot!
7 They would go to Spain last year.
8 I speak very well Italian.
9 The holiday begins at the tenth of May.
10 They must have strong rules in the army.
11 I saw John today morning.
12 We'll meet at Tuesday.
13 His office is at the fifth floor.
14 What's the name from his wife?
15 He phones with his girlfriend every day.
16 She bought this clothes yesterday.
17 "Here's your cup." – "Do it on my table, please."
18 Don't you work in the Queen Street?
19 I go to Cologne twice in the week.
20 We have all made different experiences.
21 "Which beer shall we buy?" – "It's equal."
22 Clean your shoes! You can't go to the party so!
23 John's a gentleman – he's so politely.
24 You must concentrate yourself more, children!
25 When was the last strong winter?
26 The daughter company is in France.
27 Germans always change British and English.
28 Isn't this a beautiful weather?
29 Would you please be so kind to open the door?
30 There were two men – the one was German, the other was English.

1 You can see him **on** television tomorrow. (9)
2 We drove to Munich **via** Frankfurt. (319)
3 The boss always **leaves** at five o'clock. (8)
4 The soldier's **hair was** too long. (311)
5 That's a very **simple** problem. (313)
6 **Whoever** said that is an idiot! (318)
7 They **wanted to** go to Spain last year. (307)
8 I speak Italian **very well**. (308)
9 The holiday begins **on** the tenth of May. (304)
10 They must have **strict** rules in the army. (302)
11 I saw John **this** morning. (299)
12 We'll meet **on** Tuesday. (306)
13 His office is **on** the fifth floor. (296)
14 What's his **wife's name**? (3)
15 He **phones** his girlfriend every day. (6)
16 She bought **these** clothes yesterday. (12)
17 "Here's your cup." – "**Put** it on my table, please." (312)
18 Don't you work in **Queen Street**? (316)
19 I go to Cologne **twice a week**. (310)
20 We have all **had** different experiences. (314)
21 "Which beer shall we buy?" – "**It doesn't matter**." (309)
22 Clean your shoes! You can't go to the party **like that**! (298)
23 John's a gentleman – he's so **polite**. (305)
24 You must **concentrate** more, children! (303)
25 When was the last **bad** winter? (301)
26 The **subsidiary** is in France. (300)
27 Germans always **mix up** British and English. (297)
28 Isn't this **beautiful weather**? (117)
29 Would you please be so kind **as** to open the door? (315)
30 There were two men – **one** was German, the other was English. (317)

1 We return at the eleventh of September.
2 I like Monika – she's so kindly.
3 He would buy a new car last summer.
4 They speak very well Portuguese.
5 We made a bad experience during our holiday last year.
6 "Here's your book." – "Do it on the table, please."
7 I live in the Prince Street.
8 Who plays poker well must be a gangster!
9 That isn't a heavy problem.
10 How many milk do we need for the weekend?
11 She spent an hour to cook the meal.
12 We took the Lufthansa machine.
13 I phoned with them last Friday.
14 My hairs are too long.
15 This machines were made in Germany.
16 I can't concentrate myself so late in the evening.
17 I return at Friday.
18 She visits her family once in the week.
19 "Which one shall I take?" – "It's equal".
20 He was in television yesterday.
21 Would you please be so kind to close the window?
22 I saw two cars – the one was a Rolls Royce, the other a Jaguar.
23 You can drive to Berlin about Magdeburg.
24 He speaks good.
25 Kaufhof is a warehouse.
26 She work very hard.
27 The German police is always friendly.
28 Perfume is something the women use.
29 Here's the house from the Browns.
30 A ring is a jewellery you wear on your finger.

1 We return **on** the eleventh of September. (304)
2 I like Monika – she's so **kind**. (305)
3 He **wanted to** buy a new car last summer. (307)
4 They speak very **good** Portuguese. (308)
5 We **had** a bad experience during our holiday last year. (314)
6 "Here's your book." – "**Put** it on the table, please." (312)
7 I live in **Prince Street**. (316)
8 **Anybody that** plays poker well must be a gangster! (318)
9 That isn't a **difficult** problem. (313)
10 How **much** milk do we need for the weekend? (320)
11 She spent an hour **cooking** the meal. (323)
12 We took the Lufthansa **flight**. (324)
13 I **phoned** them last Friday. (6)
14 My **hair is** too long. (311)
15 **These** machines were made in Germany. (12)
16 I can't **concentrate** so late in the evening. (303)
17 I return **on** Friday. (306)
18 She visits her family **once a week**. (310)
19 "Which one shall I take?" – "**It doesn't matter**". (309)
20 He was **on** television yesterday. (9)
21 Would you please be so kind **as** to close the window? (315)
22 I saw two cars – **one** was a Rolls Royce, the other a Jaguar. (317)
23 You can drive to Berlin **via** Magdeburg. (319)
24 He speaks **well**. (322)
25 Kaufhof is a **department store**. (321)
26 She **works** very hard. (8)
27 The German police **are** always friendly. (325)
28 Perfume is something **women** use. (326)
29 Here's the **Browns' house**. (3)
30 A ring is **a piece of** jewellery you wear on your finger. (117)

1 The British Airways machine was late.
2 I spent two hours to do the work.
3 I think the British police is wonderful!
4 Do you like a coffee?
5 She's the onliest woman I have ever loved.
6 My wife and I do the homework together.
7 I remember the time where I was poor.
8 Diamonds are something for the women.
9 Does she make her work well?
10 John is so big as Nigel.
11 Sorry? How was your name?
12 Did you phone to Jim yesterday?
13 Give me that books, please.
14 He always come before eight o'clock.
15 They play some good music in the radio.
16 There's the cat from the neighbours.
17 I have an information for you.
18 My hairs were fairer when I was younger.
19 He flies to the USA once in the year.
20 It isn't light to get tickets for the show.
21 "Here's the film." – "Do it in the camera, please."
22 She made a bad experience when she was abroad.
23 Two men died – the one was French, the other Swedish.
24 Peter has a shop in the Crown Street.
25 "What's the best route to Munich?" – "Over Stuttgart."
26 Would you please be so kind to send me the money?
27 Who drives a Ferrari must have money.
28 Did you have many rain during your holiday?
29 She swims good.
30 The nearest warehouse is Horten.

1 The British Airways **flight** was late. (324)
2 I spent two hours **doing** the work. (323)
3 I think the British police **are** wonderful! (325)
4 **Would** you like a coffee? (327)
5 She's the **only** woman I have ever loved. (328)
6 My wife and I do the **housework** together. (329)
7 I remember the time **when** I was poor. (330)
8 Diamonds are something for **women**. (326)
9 Does she **do** her work well? (267)
10 John is **as** big **as** Nigel. (331)
11 Sorry? **What** was your name? (332)
12 Did you **phone** Jim yesterday? (6)
13 Give me **those** books, please. (12)
14 He always **comes** before eight o'clock. (8)
15 They play some good music **on** the radio. (9)
16 There's the **neighbours' cat**. (3)
17 I have **some** information for you. (117)
18 My **hair was** fairer when I was younger. (311)
19 He flies to the USA **once a year**. (310)
20 It isn't **easy** to get tickets for the show. (313)
21 "Here's the film." – "**Put** it in the camera, please." (312)
22 She **had** a bad experience when she was abroad. (314)
23 Two men died – **one** was French, the other Swedish. (317)
24 Peter has a shop in **Crown Street**. (316)
25 "What's the best route to Munich?" – "**Via** Stuttgart." (319)
26 Would you please be so kind **as** to send me the money? (315)
27 **Anybody that** drives a Ferrari must have money. (318)
28 Did you have **much** rain during your holiday? (320)
29 She swims **well**. (322)
30 The nearest **department store** is Horten. (321)

1 The Italian police is very charming.
2 I phoned to Jane yesterday.
3 Who? I?
4 Our son has three hours' housework every day.
5 She's the wife of John.
6 That's an interesting news.
7 How much cars have they got?
8 How is your name, please?
9 They play good.
10 The Indians mustn't cry!
11 A plate is a thing where we eat from.
12 Show me that photos, please.
13 She never arrive on time.
14 Do you like a beer?

15 The window is so high as the door.
16 Please may I see the photo?
17 He has driven with the car to Bremen twice this year.
18 Who lives in the slums must be poor.
19 "What did you do last night?" – "I read in my book."
20 Chablis is the onliest wine I drink.
21 Wasn't that the time where they lived here?
22 "Why didn't you tell me that Smith is ill?" – "I didn't know it."
23 Two women came in – the one was poor, the other was rich.
24 What time does the Air France machine land?
25 We must make a lot of work in the office.
26 Which is the better warehouse – Horten or Karstadt?
27 He normally spends half an hour to write to her.
28 He's reading the paper in the moment.
29 I listened to the news in the radio yesterday.
30 "What's the best route to Heidelberg?" – "About Mannheim."

1 The Italian police **are** very charming. (325)

2 I **phoned** Jane yesterday. (6)

3 Who? **Me**? (333)

4 Our son has three hours' **homework** every day. (329)

5 She's **John's wife**. (3)

6 That's **interesting news**. (117)

7 How **many** cars have they got? (320)

8 **What** is your name, please? (332)

9 They play **well**. (322)

10 **Indians** mustn't cry! (326)

11 A plate is a **thing we** eat from. (7)

12 Show me **those** photos, please. (12)

13 She never **arrives** on time. (8)

14 **Would** you like a beer? (327)

15 The window is **as** high **as** the door. (331)

16 May I see the photo, **please**? (4)

17 He **has driven** to Bremen twice this year. (5)

18 **Anybody that** lives in the slums must be poor. (318)

19 "What did you do last night?" – "I **read** my book." (1)

20 Chablis is the **only** wine I drink. (328)

21 Wasn't that the time **when** they lived here? (330)

22 "Why didn't you tell me that Smith is ill?" – "I didn't **know**." (2)

23 Two women came in – **one** was poor, the other was rich. (317)

24 What time does the Air France **plane** land? (324)

25 We must **do** a lot of work in the office. (267)

26 Which **department store** is better – Horten or Karstadt? (321)

27 He normally spends half an hour **writing** to her. (323)

28 He's reading the paper **at** the moment. (11)

29 I listened to the news **on** the radio yesterday. (9)

30 "What's the best route to Heidelberg?" – "**Via** Mannheim." (319)

1 Mein Freund gab mir einen guten Rat.
2 Das ist die neue Sekretärin vom Chef.
3 Ich sah zwei Frauen – die eine war jung, die andere alt.
4 Wer das sagt, ist kein Freund von mir!
5 Können wir Chemnitz über Halle erreichen?
6 Wieviele Männer arbeiten hier?
7 Im Warenhaus gibt's ein Restaurant.
8 Sie schreibt gut.
9 Ich verbrachte eine Stunde damit, den Brief zu schreiben.
10 Die Maschine landete um acht Uhr.
11 Die Polizei ist immer freundlich.
12 Mädchen sind immer ruhiger als Jungen.
13 Möchten Sie ein Steak?
14 Pavarotti ist für mich der einzige Tenor.
15 Meine Tochter macht ihre Hausaufgaben bei ihrer Freundin.
16 Ich meine, er macht seine Arbeit gut.
17 Das war die Zeit, wo das Leben einfacher war.
18 Das Radio war so teuer wie der Videorecorder.
19 Wie ist sein Name?
20 Nein, nicht ich! Er, mit dem Hund!
21 Eine Gabel ist ein Gegenstand, mit dem man ißt.
22 Er kommt nie zu spät.
23 Hast du gestern die neue Show im Fernsehen gesehen?
24 Ich habe gestern abend in meinem neuen Buch gelesen.
25 „Weißt du, daß wir uns morgen treffen?" – „Ja, ich weiß es."
26 Er ist im Moment sehr beschäftigt.
27 Könnten Sie bitte das Fenster schließen?
28 Ich fahre viel mit dem Wagen.
29 Gib mir bitte diese Bücher.
30 Du mußt morgen deine Mutter anrufen.

1 My friend gave me good advice. (117)
2 That's the boss's new secretary. (3)
3 I saw two women – one was young, the other old. (317)
4 Whoever says that is no friend of mine! (318)
5 Can we get to Chemnitz via Halle? (319)
6 How many men work here? (320)
7 There's a restaurant in the department store. (321)
8 She writes well. (322)
9 I spent an hour writing the letter. (323)
10 The plane landed at eight o'clock. (324)
11 The police are always friendly. (325)
12 Girls are always quieter than boys. (326)
13 Would you like a steak? (327)
14 Pavarotti is the only tenor for me. (328)
15 My daughter does her homework at her friend's. (329)
16 I think he does his work well. (267)
17 That was the time when life was simpler. (330)
18 The radio was as expensive as the video-recorder. (331)
19 What's his name? (332)
20 No, not me! Him, with the dog! (333)
21 A fork is a thing you eat with. (7)
22 He never comes late. (8)
23 Did you watch the new show on television yesterday? (9)
24 I read my new book yesterday evening. (1)
25 "Do you know that we are meeting tomorrow" – "Yes, I know." (2)
26 He's very busy at the moment. (11)
27 Could you close the window, please? (4)
28 I drive a lot. (5)
29 Give me those books, please. (12)
30 You must phone your mother tomorrow. (6)

1 Please may we take the car tonight?
2 That papers are mine.
3 He's drinking coffee in the moment.
4 I remember the time where he was a nobody.
5 Do you like a cup of tea?
6 They are so intelligent people.
7 We heard him in the radio on Saturday.
8 I drive a lot with the car.
9 How is your sister's name?
10 I've never made so much work in my life!
11 The boys everywhere are noisy.
12 The French police works well.
13 A warehouse is the best place to buy a present.
14 John's got a new car. Did you know this?
15 The teacher makes them do a lot of housework.
16 He was reading in his book when she arrived.
17 I don't know how they call that in English.
18 They dance good.
19 It work perfectly.
20 He phoned to his girlfriend from his office.
21 Tennis is the onliest sport he likes.
22 The cat is so heavy as the dog.
23 I bought this book by Kaufhof.
24 It's the book of the secretary.
25 Did you see much birds in the forest?
26 A desk is an object where you work at.
27 Who? We?
28 They spent three days with trying to do it.
29 I have another luggage here.
30 What time does the SAS machine land?

1 May we take the car tonight, **please**? (4)
2 **Those** papers are mine. (12)
3 He's drinking coffee **at** the moment. (11)
4 I remember the time **when** he was a nobody. (330)
5 **Would** you like a cup of tea? (327)
6 They are **such** intelligent people. (14)
7 We heard him **on** the radio on Saturday. (9)
8 I **drive** a lot. (5)
9 **What** is your sister's name? (332)
10 I've never **done** so much work in my life! (267)
11 **Boys** everywhere are noisy. (326)
12 The French police **work** well. (325)
13 A **department store** is the best place to buy a present. (321)
14 John's got a new car. Did you know **that**? (2)
15 The teacher makes them do a lot of **homework**. (329)
16 He was **reading** his book when she arrived. (1)
17 I don't know **what** they call that in English. (10)
18 They dance **well**. (322)
19 It **works** perfectly. (8)
20 He **phoned** his girlfriend from his office. (6)
21 Tennis is the **only** sport he likes. (328)
22 The cat is **as** heavy **as** the dog. (331)
23 I bought this book **at** Kaufhof. (13)
24 It's the **secretary's book**. (3)
25 Did you see **many** birds in the forest? (320)
26 A desk is an **object** you work at. (7)
27 Who? **Us**? (333)
28 They spent three days **trying** to do it. (323)
29 I have another **piece of** luggage here. (117)
30 What time does the SAS **plane** land? (324)

1 China has more than one billion people. Did you know this?
2 If he would know the answer, he would win.
3 What's the opposite from cheap?
4 She starts work by Rank Xerox on Monday.
5 The shoes are of leather.
6 "What was she doing?" – "She was reading in her book."
7 I must phone to her tomorrow.
8 The museum was a great, ugly building.
9 I would like to marry in Scotland.
10 She sometimes phone me.
11 Lufthansa has lost a luggage.
12 Please can I have a cigarette?
13 Not I! He! The one in red!
14 Do you like an ice-cream?
15 She drove to Oxford with the car.
16 How is your Christian name, please?
17 Enrico is the onliest Italian we know.
18 Can you see that people over there?
19 Had you birthday last week?
20 That was the time where we were in Spain.
21 They're watching television in the moment.
22 That's the dog of the Smiths.
23 A pen is an object where you write with.
24 It's so a difficult job.
25 Are you making a lot of work at the moment?
26 I heard the report in the radio last week.
27 That's something what we need.
28 The teacher wants the children to do more housework.
29 Do you know how they call "window" in French?
30 Your car is so fast as mine.

1 China has more than one billion people. Did you know **that**? (2)

2 If he **knew** the answer, he would win. (15)

3 What's the opposite **of** cheap? (18)

4 She starts work **at** Rank Xerox on Monday. (13)

5 The shoes are **made** of leather. (16)

6 "What was she doing?" – "She was **reading** her book." (1)

7 I must **phone** her tomorrow. (6)

8 The museum was a **big**, ugly building. (20)

9 I would like to **get married** in Scotland. (21)

10 She sometimes **phones** me. (8)

11 Lufthansa has lost **some** luggage. (117)

12 Can I have a cigarette, **please**? (4)

13 Not **Me**! **Him**! The one in red! (333)

14 **Would** you like an ice-cream? (327)

15 She **drove** to Oxford. (5)

16 **What** is your Christian name, please? (332)

17 Enrico is the **only** Italian we know. (328)

18 Can you see **those** people over there? (12)

19 **Was it your** birthday last week? (19)

20 That was the time **when** we were in Spain. (330)

21 They're watching television **at** the moment. (11)

22 That's the **Smiths' dog**. (3)

23 A pen is an **object you** write with. (7)

24 It's **such** a difficult job. (14)

25 Are you **doing** a lot of work at the moment? (267)

26 I heard the report **on** the radio last week. (9)

27 That's **something we** need. (17)

28 The teacher wants the children to do more **homework**. (329)

29 Do you know **what** they call "window" in French? (10)

30 Your car is **as** fast **as** mine. (331)

Grammar

1 Es heißt nicht **I was reading in the book**, sondern **I was reading the book**.

2 Man sagt entweder **I (don't) know** oder **I (don't) know that**. Die Formen **I (don't) know this** und **I (don't) know it** sind ungebräuchlich.

3 Wenn Dinge im Genitiv benutzt werden, sagt man z.B. **the leg of the table**, aber bei Personen und Tieren heißt es **the teacher's leg / the cat's leg** (**from** ist hier falsch).

4 **Please** am Anfang einer Bitte betont diese zu sehr. Die normale Position ist am Ende des Satzes.

5 Die übliche Bedeutung von **to drive** ist „mit dem Wagen fahren".

6 Hinter dem Verb **to phone** steht keine Präposition (Verhältniswort). Man sagt niemals **to phone with** oder **to phone to**.

7 In den unten angegebenen Konstruktionen darf man **where** nicht benutzen. **Which** kann verwendet werden; der Verzicht auf das Relativpronomen (bezügliches Fürwort) ist jedoch sprachlich besser.

A plate is a thing where we eat from. (falsch)
A plate is a thing which we eat from. (korrektes Englisch)
A plate is a thing we eat from. (gutes, gebräuchliches Englisch)

8 Die dritte Person Singular Präsens (Gegenwart) endet auf '**s**', z.B. **he speaks, she reads**.

9 Die korrekte Präposition (Verhältniswort) für Radio und Fernsehen ist **on**, nicht **in**, z.B. **I saw it on television**.

10 Man sagt nicht **How do you call that?**, sondern **What do you call that?**

11 Es heißt nicht **in the moment**, sondern **at the moment**.

12 Viele Lernende vergessen, daß **this** und **that** die Pluralformen (Mehrzahl) **these** und **those** haben.

13 Ein „Deutsch-Englisch"-Fehler ist es, wenn man „bei" mit **by** übersetzt. **At** oder **for** wäre korrekt im Englischen.

14 Vor einer Konstruktion mit Adjektiv + Substantiv (Eigenschaftswort + Hauptwort) benutzt man **such (a / an)**, z.B. **It's such a beautiful day** oder **They're such charming people**. Vor einem Adjektiv benutzt man **so**, z.B. **It's so beautiful** oder **They are so nice**.

15 Die normale Konstruktion in einem Bedingungssatz (Typ 2) ist: **If** + Imperfekt (Vergangenheit), **would** + Infinitiv, z.B. **If I went to England, I would visit London**, nicht **If I would go to England, I would visit London**.

16 Ein weiterer „Deutsch-Englisch"-Fehler: „Der Tisch ist aus Holz" ist **The table is made of wood**.

17 Es heißt nicht **something what**, sondern **something that** oder **something which**, z.B. **That's something that we don't need** oder **That's something which we don't need**.

18 Auf **opposite** folgt **of**, nicht **from**.

19 Ein „Deutsch-Englisch"-Fehler – statt **I have birthday in May** sagt man **It's my birthday in May** oder **My birthday is in May**.

20 **Great** bedeutet normalerweise **wonderful** oder **fantastic**.

21 In der Konversation ist die Form **We got married in May** gebräuchlicher als **We married in May**.

22 In einem Affirmativsatz (bejahender Satz) sollte man **a lot of**, und nicht **much** oder **many** verwenden, z.B. **He's got a lot of money**.

23 Auf bestimmte Verben (**to want, tell, like, expect** etc.) folgt die Konstruktion Akkusativ + Infinitiv (Wenfall + Grundform), z.B. **I want them to help me**, nicht **I want that they help me**.

24 „Es gibt" wird im Englischen mit **there is / are** übersetzt.

25 Die Form **that what** existiert im Englischen nicht. Vergessen Sie das **that**, und der Satz ist korrekt.

26 **I think that ...** bedeutet „Ich meine / glaube, daß ...“. **I mean that ...** bedeutet „Ich will sagen, daß ...“.

27 Für Englischsprechende ist **a house** normalerweise ein Wohnhaus.

28 Deutsche Fragesätze des Typs „In welchem Krankenhaus ist sie?“ werden in der englischen Umgangssprache anders konstruiert. Man beginnt mit dem Fragewort (**what, which, who** etc.) und endet mit der Präposition (**with, in, to** etc.), z.B. **Which hospital is she in?**

29 **The most people** ist nicht korrekt. Es muß heißen **most people**.

30 In einer passiven Konstruktion muß man **by** (nicht **from**) benutzen, z.B. „eingeladen von“ ist **invited by**.

31 **Have you to do it?** ist die veraltete Form. Üblich sind: **Do you have to do it? – Yes, I do / No, I don't** oder **Did you have to do it? – Yes, I did / No, I didn't**.

32 **At this time** bedeutet immer „jetzt / in diesem Moment“. Wenn man über die Vergangenheit sprechen will, sagt man **at that time**.

33 Ein „Deutsch-Englisch“-Fehler – man sagt **I met her at the party** und nicht **I met her on the party**.

34 **To bring** bedeutet „hierherbringen“. **To take** bedeutet „hinbringen / wegbringen“.

35 Im Englischen sagt man nicht **We see us tomorrow**, sondern **(I will) See you tomorrow**.

36 Wenn es unsicher ist, ob eine Handlung stattfindet, wird **if** benutzt. Man sagt **when**, wenn es feststeht, daß ein Ereignis eintrifft, aber der Zeitpunkt ungewiß ist.

37 Verwechseln Sie nicht:

stay, stayed, stayed = bleiben
stand, stood, stood = stehen

38 Man übt eine Sprache oder ein Musikinstrument **(practise)**. Man trainiert eine Fußballmannschaft **(train)**.

39 Ein „Deutsch-Englisch"-Fehler – korrekt ist **the same as**, nicht **the same like**.

40 In dem Ausdruck **a two-day trip** ist **two-day** ein Adjektiv (Eigenschaftswort), ähnlich wie **long** oder **short**. Genauso wie es nicht möglich ist, **a longs trip** oder **a shorts trip** zu sagen, ist es falsch, von **a two-days trip** zu reden.

41 Viel gebräuchlicher als **to inform oneself** ist der Ausdruck **to find out**.

42 „Auch" kann mit **too**, **as well** oder **also** übersetzt werden. Normalerweise stehen **too** und **as well** am Ende des Satzes, z.B. **They speak English, too / They speak English as well**. **Also** steht direkt vor dem Verb (Tätigkeitswort), z.B. **They also speak English**. Eine Ausnahme ist **to be** – **also** steht hinter **to be**, z.B. **They are also English**.

43 Nach **it's (not) worth ...** „es lohnt sich (nicht), ..." wird das Gerundium (die ...ing-Form) benutzt, z.B. **It's not worth buying a fridge in Alaska**.

44 In einem Satz wie **He bought a cake to eat it** beziehen sich **cake** und **it** auf dasselbe Objekt – es ist „doppelt gemoppelt". Korrekt ist **He bought a cake to eat**.

45 „Ostern" ist im Englischen **Easter**, und nicht **Eastern**.

46 **Most time(s)** muß eine verdeutschte Version von **mostly** sein. Gebräuchlicher als **mostly** ist **normally** oder **usually**.

47 Die Kurzform von **at the age of twenty** ist **at twenty** und nicht **with twenty**.

48 Ein Verbrecher kommt ins Gefängnis / ist im Gefängnis (**goes to prison / is in prison**). Seine Familie geht ins Gefängnis / ist im Gefängnis (**goes to the prison / is in the prison**), um ihn zu besuchen. Derselbe Unterschied gilt bei anderen Institutionen, z.B. **school, hospital, church** etc.

49 Verwechseln Sie nicht:

die, died, died = sterben
dead = tot
death = Tod

50 **Trousers** (Hose), **scissors** (Schere), **glasses** (Brille) stehen immer im Plural (Mehrzahl) und brauchen daher auch Plural-Verbformen.

51 „Worauf (Auf was) stellen Sie die Tasse?“ ist im Englischen **What do you put the cup on?**, nicht **Where do you put the cup on?** Ähnlich:

„Worin (In was) …?“ ist **What … in?**
„Womit (Mit was) …?“ ist **What … with?**

52 Für Briten ist **backside** (Hintern) der Teil des Körpers, auf dem man sitzt. „Rückseite“ ist **back** im britischen Englisch.

53 „Hunger / Durst haben“ heißt **to be hungry / thirsty**.

54 **Any, anything, anybody** werden in Interrogativ(Frage-)sätzen und Negativ(Verneinungs-)sätzen benutzt; **some, something, somebody** in Affirmativ(Bejahungs-)sätzen.

55 In einem englischen Satz ist die Wortstellung normalerweise Subjekt – Prädikat (Satzaussage) – Objekt. Das Adverb (Umstandswort) **there** steht nach dem Objekt, z.B. **You can eat Italian food there**, nicht **You can eat there Italian food**.

56 „In letzter Zeit“ heißt **lately** oder **recently**.

57 „In nächster Zeit“ heißt **in the near future**.

58 Man muß vorsichtig sein mit den fünf Verben der Sinne (**to feel, taste, smell, sound, look**). **Mary smells good** bedeutet, daß sie ein gutes Parfüm benutzt. **Mary smells well** bedeutet, daß sie eine gute Nase hat, und (zum Beispiel) einen französischen und einen italienischen Wein allein auf Grund des Geruchs unterscheiden kann.

59 **For this reason** hört sich in der Umgangssprache etwas steif an. Viel besser ist **(and) that's why** oder **(and) so**.

60 Die gängige Geburtstagsgratulation ist **Happy Birthday!**

61 **A photo from my cat** bedeutet, daß meine Katze mir ein Foto gegeben hat. **A photo of my cat** ist ein Foto, auf dem man meine Katze sehen kann.

62 Englischsprechende benutzen sehr selten die Formen **too few / too little** (zu wenig). Sie bevorzugen es, den Satz zu verneinen, indem sie **not enough** (nicht genug) verwenden, z.B. **We haven't got enough coffee for the weekend**.

63 „Einmal" ist **once**, „zweimal" ist **twice**.

64 „Ein Freund von mir / dir / ihm etc." heißt **a friend of mine / yours / his** etc., nicht **a friend of me / you / him** etc.

65 Man darf nicht das „End-s" vergessen, wenn man **sport** als Adjektiv (Eigenschaftswort) verwendet, z.B. **a sports car**, nicht **a sport car**.

66 **The both men** ist im Englischen nicht richtig. Korrekt ist **both men** oder **the two men**.

67 „Eine Frau" ist **a woman**, aber „eine Ehefrau" ist **a wife**.

68 **To become** heißt „werden", **to get** heißt „bekommen".

69 Die Plural(Mehrzahl-)form **knowledges** existiert im Englischen nicht, und der Singular (Einzahl) **knowledge** wird selten verwendet. Viel besser als **I have some knowledge of French** ist **I know a little French** oder **I speak a little French**.

70 Nach dem Wort **hundred** sollte man **and** sagen, z.B. **one hundred and one**.

71 Vor einem Substantiv (Hauptwort) muß die Adjektivform (Eigenschaftswort) **real** verwendet werden, z.B. **a real problem** (ein echtes Problem).

72 Das Verb (Tätigkeitswort) **to catch** ist unregelmäßig: **catch, caught, caught.**

73 Normalerweise wird bei einem Sportresultat die höhere Zahl zuerst genannt. Falls es notwendig ist, wird der Name der

Mannschaft ebenfalls angegeben, z.B. **two-one for Stuttgart, three-two for Munich**. In den meisten Sportarten verwendet man **nil** für „null". Tennis und Tischtennis sind Ausnahmen – in diesen Sportarten heißt es **love**.

74 „Platz" im Sinne von „Platzangebot" wird im Englischen mit **room** übersetzt.

75 **To play** ist „spielen", aber **a play** ist „ein Theaterstück". Es heißt **game** oder **match**, wenn man über Sport spricht, z.B. **a football game, a tennis match**.

76 **Shadow**, als optischer Begriff, bezieht sich auf etwas, das auf dem Boden oder an der Wand zu erkennen ist. Man verwendet das Wort **shade**, wenn von Temperatur oder Schutz vor der Sonne die Rede ist.

77 Eine Straße inmitten einer Stadt wird als **street** bezeichnet, aber zwischen zwei Städten als **road**.

78 **To be afraid** ist „Angst haben". **To be angry** ist „böse sein".

79 **I'm twenty-one years old** ist korrekt, aber nicht sehr gebräuchlich. **I'm twenty-one years** ist falsch. Normalerweise sagt man **I'm twenty-one**.

80 Die Übersetzung von „Was machen Sie?" ist **What do you do?**, nicht **What do you?** „Er macht seine Arbeit nicht gut" wird mit **He doesn't do his work well**, nicht **He doesn't his work well** übersetzt.

81 Es gibt zwei Möglichkeiten „anderthalb Stunden" zu übersetzen: **an hour and a half** oder **one and a half hours**.

82 Ein „Deutsch-Englisch"-Fehler:
lie, lay, lain = liegen
lay, laid, laid = legen
lie down, lay down, lain down = sich hinlegen

83 Es heißt nicht **What colour has the sky?**, sondern **What colour is the sky?**

84 **Persons** ist korrekt, aber **people** ist viel gängiger.

85 **Often, never, sometimes, always** etc. sind spezielle Adverbien (Umstandswörter) und sollten direkt vor dem Verb stehen, z.B. **I always drink coffee**, aber sie stehen hinter dem Verb **to be**, z.B. **He is always late**.

86 Das Adjektiv (Eigenschaftswort) **drunken** kann nur vor einem Substantiv (Hauptwort) stehen wie in dem Lied **What shall we do with the drunken sailor?** Man sagt nicht **The sailor is drunken**, sondern **The sailor is drunk**.

87 Ein „Deutsch-Englisch"-Fehler – die korrekte englische Form ist **What about a coffee?** oder **How about a coffee?**

88 Ein „Deutsch-Englisch"-Fehler – die korrekte englische Form ist **in the wild**.

89 Das deutsche Wort „direkt" im Sinne von „in unmittelbarer Nähe" wird ins Englische mit **right** übersetzt, z.B. **right behind me / right in front of you / right next to him**.

90 Dieser Fehler ist weit verbreitet und schwer auszumerzen. „Wenn er Geld machen will, muß er mehr arbeiten". Oft wird das deutsche Wort „will" (wollen) fälschlicherweise mit dem englischen **will** (werden) übersetzt. Korrekt ist **If he wants to make money, he must work more**.

91 Es wäre korrekt zu sagen **all the people**, aber **everybody** (oder **everyone**) ist moderner.

92 **All the things** ist nicht falsch, aber **everything** ist gebräuchlicher.

93 Die korrekte Präposition (Verhältniswort) für die religiösen Feiertage des Jahres ist **at**, z.B. **at Christmas, at Easter, at Whitsun** (Pfingsten).

94 Ein „Deutsch-Englisch"-Fehler – **I mustn't** bedeutet „Ich darf nicht", und **I needn't** bedeutet „Ich muß nicht" oder „Ich brauche nicht".

95 „Wasser kochen" ist **to boil water**, nicht **to cook water**.

96 Das Englische ist hier etwas komplizierter als das Deutsche: die Frage lautet **How many of you were there at the party?** (Wieviele wart ihr auf dem Fest?) und die Antwort ist **There were thirty of us there** (Wir waren zu dreißig da).

97 Ein „Deutsch-Englisch"-Fehler – die normale Wortstellung im Englischen ist Subjekt – Prädikat (Satzaussage) – Objekt. Wenn man diese in Objekt – Prädikat – Subjekt ändert, kann so etwas entstehen: **The car repairs my son** (Der Wagen repariert meinen Sohn).

98 Mit **All baby animals are sweet** meint man, jedes Tierbaby auf der Welt (ohne Ausnahme) sei süß! Wenn über eine bestimmte Gruppe von jungen Tieren gesprochen wird, verwendet man die Form **all the baby animals**, z.B. **All the baby animals here (in this zoo / in this safari park / in this shop) are exotic**.

99 Nicht **It's something other**, sondern **It's something else** oder **It's something different**.

100 Viele Deutsche verwechseln diese Verben:
to look at = sich etwas anschauen
to look for = suchen
to look after = auf etwas aufpassen

101 **Nearby the church** ist falsch. Korrekt ist **near the church** oder auch **The church is nearby** (Die Kirche ist ganz in der Nähe).

102 **In former times I worked here** ist korrektes Englisch, aber nicht sehr gebräuchlich. Es ist sehr viel besser (besonders in der Konversation), „früher" oder „in früheren Zeiten" mit **used to** zu übersetzen, z.B. **I used to work here**.

103 Ein Affirmativsatz (Bejahungssatz) wird mit **too**, und ein Negativsatz (Verneinungssatz) wird mit **either** beendet, z.B. **I like winter and I like summer, too / I don't drink beer and I don't drink wine, either**.

104 **To prove** ist beweisen, **to check** ist prüfen.

105 Ein „Deutsch-Englisch"-Fehler – „verheiratet mit" ist **married to**.

106 **Information** kann im Englischen nie im Plural stehen.

107 Im modernen Englisch verwendet man die Verben (Tätigkeitswörter) **wash / dress / shave** ohne die Reflexivpronomen (rückbezügliche Fürwörter) **myself / yourself / himself** etc. **I normally shave before breakfast** bedeutet natürlich, daß ich mich selber rasiere (nicht meinen Bruder). Der Trend geht dahin, diese drei Verben zusammen mit **to get** zu verwenden – **to get washed / to get dressed / to get shaved**.

108 Ein „Deutsch-Englisch"-Fehler – im Englischen heißt es **As a child he was brilliant**.

109 Die normale Wortstellung in einem englischen Satz ist Subjekt – Prädikat (Satzaussage) – Objekt. Es ist nicht üblich **That letter I read yesterday** zu sagen, sondern **I read that letter yesterday**.

110 Bei Betonung einer Aussage werden die Pronomen (Fürwörter) **myself / yourself / himself** etc. benutzt, z.B. **The President gave the speech himself** – „Der Präsident hielt den Vortrag selber". **The President gave the speech by himself** hat eine völlig andere Bedeutung – **by himself** bedeutet „alleine, ohne Hilfe".

111 „Reisen" ist **to travel**. Eine Reise ist **a trip**.

112 Die normale Präposition (Verhältniswort) nach **to go** ist **to**.

113 **Cry** kann „schreien" bedeuten, doch die hauptsächliche Bedeutung ist „weinen". Die beste Übersetzung von „schreien" ist **shout**.

114 **He told that he was ill** ist nicht richtig im Englischen. Nach **tell / told** muß man normalerweise den Zuhörer nennen, z.B. **He told me (us / them / his boss) that he was ill**. Man kann **say** statt **tell** benutzen, z.B. **He said that he was ill. He said to me that he was ill** ist korrekt, aber nicht sehr elegant.

115 „Ich brauchte eine Stunde, um den Brief zu schreiben" ist **It took me an hour to write the letter**.

116 Ein „Deutsch-Englisch“-Fehler – Englischsprechende beginnen einen Satz normalerweise mit **there is** oder **there are**, z.B. **There are seven rooms in the house**.

117 Manche Substantive (Hauptwörter) dürfen im Englischen niemals zusammen mit **a(n)** benutzt werden. Die gängigsten sind **weather** (Wetter), **furniture** (Möbel), **advice** (Rat), **information** (Information), **news** (Nachricht), **baggage** (Gepäck), **luggage** (Gepäck), **jewellery** (Schmuck). Manchmal treten diese Wörter zusammen mit **some** oder **a piece of** auf, z.B. **a piece of furniture / some advice**.

118 Hinter der Präposition (Verhältniswort) **during** steht normalerweise ein Substantiv (Hauptwort), z.B. **during the day / during the lesson / during our holiday**. Um zwei Sätze zusammenzufügen, wird die Konjunktion (Bindewort) **while** verwendet, z.B. **I wrote letters while he cooked the dinner** oder **Susan washed the car while John made the coffee**.

119 Ein „Deutsch-Englisch“-Fehler – „Haustier“ ist **pet** im Englischen, wenn das Tier ein „Freund/Mitglied“ der Familie ist.

120 Vor den Zahlen **hundred** und **thousand** muß **a** oder **one** stehen.

121 **Pay** ohne **for** wird nur dann benutzt, wenn ausgedrückt werden soll, daß jemand für eine Arbeit bezahlt wird, z.B. **I paid the window-cleaner yesterday**. Man sagt **pay for**, wenn es um ein Objekt geht, das man gekauft hat, z.B. **I have paid for the newspapers**.

122 **To search** ist „durchsuchen“ und **to search for** oder **to look for** ist „suchen“.

123 **Last night** ist „letzte / heute nacht“ und **tonight** ist „heute abend“.

124 **I speak only a little bit English** ist falsch. **I speak only a little bit of English** ist nicht unkorrekt, jedoch ist **I speak only a little English** viel besser.

125 „Größer als“ ist **bigger than**, nicht **bigger as**.

126 **My daughter she is nice** – diese umgangssprachliche Doppelform (Hauptwort und Fürwort zusammen), die im Deutschen oft benutzt wird, ist im Englischen ungebräuchlich.

127 „Ein Glas Bier“ ist **a glass of beer** und „ein Kilo Zucker“ ist **a kilo of sugar**.

128 Sportresultate werden normalerweise ohne das **to** in der Mitte angegeben.

129 Ein „Deutsch-Englisch“-Fehler – „senden“ im technischen Sinn (z.B. Fernsehen) ist **to show**.

130 Das Imperfekt (Vergangenheit) von **must** ist **had to** (mußte(n)).

131 Im Zusamenhang mit Kleidung wird **to put on** (anziehen) und **to take off** (ausziehen) benutzt.

132 Ein „Deutsch-Englisch“-Fehler – für einen Test bekommt man **a mark**, nicht **a note. Note** ist entweder eine „Banknote“, eine „Note in der Musik“ oder eine „Notiz“.

133 Ein „Deutsch-Englisch“-Fehler – „im Krankenhaus liegen“ ist **to be in hospital**.

134 Es heißt nicht **let me alone**, sondern **leave me alone**. Die Bedeutung von **to let** ist „erlauben, gestatten“ (**to allow, permit**).

135 Als Regel sagt man **made of**, wenn die Originalsubstanz noch zu erkennen ist, z.B. **The window is made of glass** (man kann das Glas noch erkennen). Wenn sich die Originalsubstanz in etwas völlig anderes verändert hat (was oft der Fall bei Dingen ist, die man ißt oder trinkt), wird **made from** benutzt, z.B. **Wine is made from grapes** (Trauben) oder **Cheese is made from milk**.

136 Ein „Deutsch-Englisch“-Fehler – „Was haben Sie?“ ist:
What's wrong with you? oder
What's the matter with you? oder
What's up with you?

137 Ein „Deutsch-Englisch“-Fehler – „einen Fehler machen“ ist **to make a mistake**, nicht **to do a mistake**.

138 Kleidungsstücke sollten zusammen mit den Possessivadjektiven (besitzanzeigende Eigenschaftswörter) **my / your / his / her / our / their** benutzt werden, z.B. **my hat, your shoes** etc.

139 „Sollen" im Sinne von „Man sagt ..." ist **to be supposed to...** . **Rolls Royce is supposed to be the best car in the world** bedeutet **People say Rolls Royce is the best car in the world** oder **I have heard Rolls Royce is the best car in the world**.

140 Eine spontane Ankündigung, daß jemand gewillt ist, etwas zu tun, muß mit **will** gebildet werden, z.B. **Who can help me? – I'll help you**, nicht **I help you**.

141 Die Präposition (Verhältniswort) **before** wird verwendet, wenn über Zeit gesprochen wird, z.B. **before twelve o'clock, before the holiday** etc. Wenn ein Ort (Position) gemeint ist, sagt man **in front of**, z.B. **She waited for John in front of the cinema**.

142 Körperteile sollten zusammen mit den Possessivadjektiven (besitzanzeigende Eigenschaftswörter) **my / your / his / her / our / their** benutzt werden, z.B. **She cut her hand with a knife**.

143 Das Possessivpronomen **it** wird benutzt in **The dog broke its leg**, wenn ausgedrückt werden soll, daß keine enge Beziehung zu dem Tier besteht. Andernfalls heißt es **he** oder **she**, z.B. **My dog Prince broke his leg**.

144 Ein „Deutsch-Englisch"-Fehler – „alle zwei Minuten" ist **every two minutes**.

145 Ein „Deutsch-Englisch"-Fehler – „bekleidet mit" ist **dressed in**.

146 Wenn man über eine Jahreszahl spricht, wird normalerweise **hundred and** ausgelassen, z.B. **I was born in nineteen seventy (1970)**, nicht **nineteen hundred and seventy**.

147 „Recht haben" ist **to be right**, nicht **to have right**, z.B. **You are right – it is a Rolls Royce**.

148 Ein „Deutsch-Englisch"-Fehler – „Das ist unterschiedlich" ist **It varies** oder **It depends**.

149 **Ill** ist eines jener Adjektive (Eigenschaftswörter), die nicht vor einem Substantiv (Hauptwort) stehen dürfen. Es heißt nicht **He is an ill man**, korrekt ist **He is ill** oder **He is a sick man**.

150 „Eine Schule besuchen“ ist **to go to a school** oder manchmal **to attend a school**. Im Zusammenhang mit Kino / Theater / Oper / Konzert heißt es **to go to**.

151 Im Englischen verwendet man oft **What ... like?**, eine sehr gebräuchliche und wichtige Redewendung, um „Wie ... ?“ zu übersetzen, z.B.

Wie war der Film? = **What was the film like?**
Wie ist seine Frau? = **What is his wife like?**
Wie war der Urlaub? = **What was the holiday like?**

152 Es heißt **next** im chronologischen Sinn (**next week / month / year** etc.), oder wenn man von Dingen spricht, die in einer geraden Linie angeordnet sind: **The Browns live in the next house, and the Smiths live in the next one (after the Browns)**. **Next** bedeutet „der, die, das nächste (folgende)“, **nearest** bedeutet „der, die, das nächstliegende“.

153 Ein „Deutsch-Englisch“-Fehler – „Schlafzimmer“ ist **bedroom**.

154 **Each** ist in diesen Sätzen möglich, aber **every** ist gebräuchlicher.

155 Ein sehr verbreiteter Fehler – korrekt ist: **I have / you have / he (she, it) has / we have / they have**.

156 Ein „Deutsch-Englisch“-Fehler – „Er hat eine eigene Wohnung“ ist **He has a flat of his own** oder **He has his own flat**.

157 Ein „Deutsch-Englisch“-Fehler – „Er ist beim Metzger“ ist **He's at the butcher's (shop)**. Genauso sagt man **at his mother's (house / flat / home)** oder **at the lawyer's (practice)**.

158 Ein „Deutsch-Englisch“-Fehler – „Urlaub machen“ ist **to have / take / spend my (your / his / her / our / their) holiday(s)** oder **to go on holiday**.

159 **Meaning** ist „Bedeutung“; **opinion** ist „Meinung“.

160 „Denken an“ ist **to think of / about**.

161 „Ich interessiere mich für Musik" ist **I'm interested in music**, nicht **I'm interested for music**.

162 „... alles, was ..." ist **... everything (that) ...**, z.B. **I heard everything (that) they said**.

163 Die Kurzform von **I'll try to do it** ist **I'll try**, nicht **I'll try it**.

164 **Until** und **till** bedeuten „die ganze Zeit bis"; **by** bedeutet „bis spätestens". **I worked till five o'clock** (Ich arbeitete [die ganze Zeit] bis fünf Uhr), aber **The money must be here by five o'clock** (Das Geld muß bis [spätestens] fünf Uhr hier sein).

165 „Jemanden daran erinnern, etwas zu tun" ist **to remind somebody to do something**. „Sich an etwas erinnern" ist **to remember something**.

166 Ein „Deutsch-Englisch"-Fehler – „in den vierziger Jahren" ist **in the forties**, nicht **in the forty years**.

167 Es heißt nicht **on the airport / fair / exhibition**, sondern **at the airport / fair / exhibition**.

168 **I think it won't rain tomorrow** ist ungewöhnlich. Sehr viel gebräuchlicher ist **I don't think it will rain tomorrow**.

169 Im Zusammenhang mit „Arbeit" wird kein Artikel benutzt, z.B. **after work**, nicht **after the work**, und **start / finish work**, nicht **start / finish the work**.

170 **Noon** und **midday** bedeuten **at twelve o'clock**. Der Ausdruck **lunch-time** ist nicht so spezifisch und wird häufiger verwendet.

171 „Ins Bett gehen" ist **to go to bed**, nicht **to go to the bed**.

172 Jemand, der kein Geld hat, muß sich welches „borgen / ausleihen" (**to borrow**); jemand, der viel Geld hat, kann welches „verleihen" (**to lend**).

173 Das Verb (Tätigkeitswort) **to rise** ist intransitiv (nichtzielend / es hat kein Objekt) – **The sun rises** oder **The house prices have risen**. Das Verb **to raise** ist transitiv (zielend / es hat ein Objekt) – **I raised my hand** oder **They have raised the prices**.

174 **The economic situation / factor** wird mit „wirtschaftlicher Situation / Faktor" übersetzt. Wenn ausgedrückt werden soll, daß ein Objekt „sparsam" ist, muß es **economical** heißen, z.B. **Little cars are very economical**.

175 „Jemandem etwas erklären" ist **to explain something to somebody**.

176 Auf das Verb (Tätigkeitswort) **to arrive** folgt normalerweise die Präposition (Verhältniswort) **at / in**, allerdings nicht zusammen mit dem Wort **home** – **to arrive home** ist eine Ausnahme.

177 In einem englischen Satz steht der Zeitausdruck üblicherweise am Ende des Satzes – **I did the work yesterday**. Wenn die Zeit aus irgendeinem Grund betont werden soll, wird sie an den Anfang des Satzes gestellt – **Yesterday I did the work**.

178 „Der, die, das gleiche wie" ist **the same as**.

179 „Er hat es alleine gemacht" ist **He did it alone / on his own / by himself**.

180 Das englische Gegenstück des deutschen umgangssprachlichen Ausdrucks „... oder so" ist **... or somebody / something / somewhere like that**.

181 „Glücklich sein" ist **to be happy**. „Glück haben" ist **to be lucky**.

182 Beachten Sie diese unregelmäßigen Mehrzahlformen: **foot / feet, child / children, man / men, woman / women**. Der normale Plural von **person** ist **people**, nicht **persons**. Man sagt **peoples** nur, wenn man Völker meint, z.B. **the peoples of the world**.

183 „Ein fünfjähriger Junge" heißt **a five-year-old boy** und nicht **a five-years-old boy**.

184 **Enough** steht direkt vor dem Substantiv (Hauptwort), z.B. **enough money, enough time**, aber nach einem Adjektiv (Eigenschaftswort), z.B. **big enough, small enough**.

185 Deutsche Fragen wie „Sie können kommen, oder?" werden im Englischen mit **'question tags'** (Frageanhängsel) gebildet. Dabei wird das Hilfsverb wiederholt, und man darf nicht

vergessen, von der bejahenden in die verneinende Form oder umgekehrt zu wechseln, z.B. **You can go, can't you? / You can't go, can you?**

186 Man sagt **the Monday** nur dann, wenn von einem ganz bestimmten Montag gesprochen wird, z.B. **I remember the Monday I started my first job**.

187 **To shout to** hat eine positive, freundliche Konnotation, z.B. **'Good morning,' he shouted to me**; **to shout at** aber eine negative, unfreundliche, z.B. **'Go away, you idiot,' he shouted at me**.

188 Hinter dem Verb (Tätigkeitswort) **to discuss** steht keine Präposition (Verhältniswort), z.B. **We discussed the new contract**, nicht **We discussed about the new contract**.

189 Ein „Deutsch-Englisch"-Fehler – „eine Art Wein" ist nicht **an art of wine**, sondern **a kind / type / sort of wine**.

190 **Run after somebody / something** bedeutet, daß man jemanden fangen will, z.B. **The policeman ran after the killer**, aber **My wife ran behind me** bedeutet, daß sie mir folgte, ohne mich fangen zu wollen.

191 „Einen Spaziergang machen" ist **to go for a walk**.

192 Die Antwort auf eine negative Frage kann **Yes** (Doch) oder **No** (Nein) sein, z.B. **Aren't you Hans Schmidt?** (Sind Sie nicht Hans Schmidt?) – **Yes, I am** (Doch, bin ich) oder **No, I'm not** (Nein, bin ich nicht).

193 „Um ... zu" ist **to**, z.B. „Ich arbeite, um Geld zu verdienen" – **I work to earn money**.

194 Ein sehr verbreiteter Fehler – man darf das Hilfsverb beim Formulieren einer Frage nicht vergessen, z.B. **What does 'table' mean in German?** (Was heißt 'table' auf deutsch?).

195 **A man** ist „ein Mann", aber **a husband** ist ein „Ehemann".

196 Im Englischen wird das Perfekt (vollendete Gegenwart) mit dem Hilfsverb **to have** gebildet. Man sagt **What has happened?**, nicht **What is happened?**

197 Ein „Deutsch-Englisch"-Fehler – „stehen" im Sinne von „aussagen / bedeuten" ist **to say**, z.B. **What does the sign say? – It says 'Welcome!'** „Stehen" kann nur dann mit **stand** übersetzt werden, wenn es die Bedeutung von 'auf den Beinen stehen' hat.

198 In der Regel ist **a town** kleiner als **a city**.

199 **Ever** hat die Bedeutung „immer" in dem Ausdruck **for ever** (für immer). Normalerweise wird **ever** mit „je / jemals / schon einmal" übersetzt, und wird in Fragen verwendet, z.B. **Have you ever visited Scotland?** Die normale Übersetzung von „immer" ist **always**.

200 Im Englischen sagt man **I need something for a headache** (gegen Kopfschmerzen).

201 Man verwendet das Wort **work** ohne **a** – natürlich kann man sagen **a job**.

202 Abstrakte Substantive (Hauptwörter), z.B. **love, hate, art** etc. werden ohne **the** verwendet.

203 Die normale Position von **every time** ist am Ende des Satzes, z.B. **He buys the same type of car every time**. Man kann aber auch **always** vor dem Verb (Tätigkeitswort) benutzen, z.B. **He always buys the same type of car**.

204 In der Konversation ist die Form **It's not green, it's yellow** gebräuchlicher als **It's not green, but yellow**.

205 Das Verb (Tätigkeitswort) **to fight** ist unregelmäßig: **fight, fought, fought**.

206 In diesem Zusammenhang heißt es **I have the work done by a gardener** (Ich lasse die Arbeit von einem Gärtner machen), und nicht **let**.

207 Viele Deutsche glauben, die Übersetzung von „Knopf" ist **buttom** (ein Wort, das im Englischen nicht existiert!) – die korrekte Übersetzung ist **button**.

208 Bevor man beginnt, jemanden zu stören heißt es **Excuse me**; wenn jemand bereits gestört wurde, **Sorry**.

209 Wein, Bier, Whisky etc. sind alkoholische Getränke (**alcoholic drinks**). **An alcoholic** ist eine Person, die regelmäßig zuviel davon trinkt (Alkoholiker).

210 Ein „Deutsch-Englisch"-Fehler – „anders als" ist **different from**.

211 Ein „Deutsch-Englisch"-Fehler – „Woher ...?" in diesem Sinn ist nicht **Where ... from?**, sondern **How ...?**, z.B. **How do you know that?** (Woher wissen Sie das?)

212 Die normale Übersetzung von „kontrollieren" ist **to check** – eine relativ kurze Aktion. **To control** ist mehr ein permanenter, ununterbrochener Vorgang, z.B. **The policemen controlled the traffic at the crossroads when the traffic-lights broke down**.

213 Ein „Deutsch-Englisch"-Fehler – „bei diesem Wetter" ist **in this / that weather**.

214 Nach Ausdrücken wie **when / if / before / after / until / till / as soon as** muß man das Präsens (Gegenwart) und nicht das Futur (Zukunft) verwenden, z.B. **We'll start when they arrive** (nicht **will arrive**).

215 **On the table** heißt „obendrauf". Die korrekte Präposition (Verhältniswort) ist hier **at**.

216 Die Pluralform (Mehrzahl) **fruits** wird sehr selten verwendet.

217 „Ich brauche nicht zu arbeiten" ist **I needn't work** oder **I don't need to work**.

218 Normalerweise benutzt man **the** nicht zusammen mit den Namen der Mahlzeiten.

219 **Congratulations!** – immer mit '**s**'.

220 „Eine Dose Farbe" wird mit **a tin of paint** übersetzt.

221 Es heißt nicht **not so ... like**, sondern **not as ... as**, z.B. **His house isn't as big as mine**.

222 Es heißt **At first ...**, wenn von zwei gegensätzlichen Dingen gesprochen wird. Normalerweise ist die Satzkonstruktion **At first ..., but then ...**, z.B. **At first the man was very friendly, but then suddenly he attacked me**. Die andere Konstruktion ist **First ..., and then ...**, z.B. **First we had dinner, and then we went for a walk**.

223 Ein „Deutsch-Englisch"-Fehler – „Es macht Spaß" ist **It's fun**.

224 Geld als gezählte Währung hat eine Mehrzahlform, z.B. **one mark, two marks / one pound, two pounds / one dollar, two dollars**.

225 Ein „Deutsch-Englisch"-Fehler – „lange schlafen" ist **to sleep in** oder **to have a lie-in**.

226 Nicht **after then**, sondern **after that**.

227 „Treffen wir uns vor dem Kino" ist **Let's meet in front of the cinema**, nicht **Let's meet us in front of the cinema**.

228 Ein „Deutsch-Englisch"-Fehler – „Ich habe mir in die Hand geschnitten" ist **I've cut my hand**.

229 Es heißt nicht **They brought the tennis yesterday**, sondern **They showed the tennis yesterday**.

230 „Ich erinnere mich an ..." ist **I remember ...**.

231 „Vor zehn Jahren" ist **ten years ago**, not **before ten years**.

232 **Who** bezieht sich auf Personen, **which** auf Objekte; **that** kann nach Personen oder Objekten verwendet werden, z.B.:

the man / woman / boy / girl who ...
the thing / object / table / book which ...
the man that ...
the book that ...

233 Man sagt **o'clock** nur bei der vollen Stunde.

234 „Etwas spendieren" ist **to buy something** im Englischen, z.B. **Let's go to the pub – I'll buy you a drink**.

235 „Glück haben" ist **to be lucky**.

236 Ein „Deutsch-Englisch“-Fehler – „Ich bin in England geboren“ ist **I was born in England**.

237 Der Himmel, den man sieht, wenn man im Freien nach oben schaut, ist **sky**. „Himmel“ im biblischen Sinne heißt **heaven**.

238 „Interessiert an“ ist **interested in**.

239 Man sagt nicht **a question to**, sondern **a question about / on**.

240 „Kaffee kochen“ ist **to make coffee**, nicht **to cook coffee**.

241 In einem englischen Satz ist die Wortstellung normalerweise Subjekt – Prädikat (Satzaussage) – Objekt. Deshalb ist es falsch zu sagen **You can find in the shop nice posters**. Korrekt ist **You can find nice posters in the shop**.

242 Die „Speisekarte“ in einem Restaurant heißt **menu**.

243 Ein „Deutsch-Englisch“-Fehler – „Ich werde morgen achtzehn“ ist **I'll be eighteen tomorrow**.

244 „Unter“ im Sinne von „zusammen mit“ ist **among**, z.B. **It's nice to be among friends**.

245 Morgens aufstehen ist **to get up**, nicht **to go up**.

246 Ein „Deutsch-Englisch“-Fehler – „gut in“ ist **good at**, z.B. **She's good at languages**.

247 **For twenty years** ist „zwanzig Jahre lang“, **twenty years ago** ist „vor zwanzig Jahren“.

248 „Einen Unterschied machen zwischen …“ ist nicht **to make a difference between …**, sondern **to distinguish between …**, z.B. **In German they don't distinguish between 'sky' and 'heaven'**.

249 Die Antriebsmaschine eines Autos ist nicht **a motor**, sondern **an engine**.

250 Man sagt nicht **double as … as**, sondern **twice as … as**.

251 Wenn von einem sozialen Ereignis (Verabredung) die Rede ist, wird **date** verwendet, für ein geschäftliches Zusammentreffen (Termin) ist **appointment** der richtige Ausdruck.

252 Diese beiden sollten nicht verwechselt werden – **beside** ist „neben“, **besides** ist „außer“ oder „außerdem“.

253 Ein sehr verbreiteter Fehler – korrekt ist: **I was / you were / he (she, it) was / we were / they were**.

254 „Sport treiben“ ist **to do sport**, nicht **to make sport**.

255 „Mittagessen“ ist **lunch** und „Abendessen“ ist **dinner**.

256 Das Wort **therefore** kann sich in einer Unterhaltung etwas steif anhören – das kleine Wort **so** klingt natürlicher.

257 Dem Ausdruck **to be used to** (gewohnt sein) muß das Gerundium (die ...ing-Form) folgen, z.B. **I am used to driving on the right** (Ich bin es gewohnt, rechts zu fahren).

258 Als Passagier mit einem Transportmittel „fahren“ heißt **to go by (bus / tram / taxi / train)**.

259 Ein „Deutsch-Englisch“-Fehler – die korrekte Zeitform im Englischen ist hier das Perfekt (vollendete Gegenwart), z.B. **I have been to England**. In einer Frage sollte das Wort **ever** (je / schon einmal) verwendet werden, z.B. **Have you ever been to England?**

260 „Sich schützen vor“ ist **to protect oneself from**, nicht **to protect oneself against**.

261 **Needn't** ist ein Hilfsverb, dem ein Vollverb folgen muß, z.B. **I needn't go** (Ich brauche nicht zu gehen). **Needn't** kann niemals zusammen mit einem Substantiv (Hauptwort) verwendet werden; so ist die Übersetzung von „Ich brauche kein Geld“ **I don't need any money**, nicht **I needn't any money**.

262 „Art zu ...“ ist **way of ...**, nicht **kind of ...**, z.B. **I like his way of talking**.

263 In der Umgangssprache verwenden Englischsprechende das 12-Stunden-Zeitsystem; sie sagen **It's ten o'clock (in the evening)**, nicht **It's twenty-two o'clock**.

264 **Of** ist nicht inkorrekt in dieser Art von Superlativsatz (höchste Steigerungsform), aber die normale Präposition (Verhältniswort) ist **in**.

265 „Autofahren“ ist **to drive a car**, aber „Fahrrad-” oder „Motorrad fahren“ ist **to ride a bike or a motorbike**.

266 Man darf hier nicht an die einzelnen, individuellen Dinge (**dollars / marks / years**) denken, sondern muß diese als Einheit sehen und deshalb ein Verb im Singular verwenden, z.B. **Six years in prison is a long time**.

267 **To do work** ist „Arbeit verrichten / tun“, **to make work** ist „Arbeit machen / verursachen“.

268 „Wie wär's mit ...?“ ist **How about ...?** oder **What about ...?**, nicht **How's about ...?** oder **What's about ...?**

269 **The film plays in America** ist sehr ungewöhnlich – viel besser ist **The film is set in America**.

270 Das Wort **chief** wird für bestimmte Titel verwendet, z.B. **Chief Constable** (ein führender Polizeibeamter), **Chief Rabbi** (der Führer einer Religionsgemeinschaft), aber normalerweise bedeutet es **Indian chief** (Häuptling).

271 Kleidungsstücke (am Körper) „tragen“ ist **to wear**, aber Dinge in der Hand oder unter dem Arm „tragen“ ist **to carry**.

272 „Eine TV-Serie“ ist **a TV series**.

273 Normalerweise steht hinter **to tell** keine Präposition (Verhältniswort), z.B. **I told her**, nicht **I told to her**.

274 Die drei Formen dieses Adjektivs (Eigenschaftswort) sind: **famous, more famous, most famous**.

275 „Mehr als“ ist **more than**, nicht **more as**.

276 **Money on the bank** bedeutet „Geld auf dem Dach der Bank“ – korrekt ist **money in the bank**.

277 Wenn das Verb (Tätigkeitswort) keine Bewegung beinhaltet, heißt es **at home**, z.B. **to stay / remain / be at home**. Wenn es sich um eine Bewegung handelt, sagt man nur **home**, z.B. **to go / come / arrive / get home**.

278 Ein „Deutsch-Englisch"-Fehler – die Übersetzung von „Was für ein Spiel ist das?" ist **What kind / type / sort of game is that?**

279 Man sollte seinen Namen nicht zusammen mit der Anrede angeben. Auf die Frage **Who's speaking, please?** wird z.B. **Schmidt speaking** oder **Schmidt here** oder **My name is Schmidt** geantwortet.

280 Wenn man gefragt wird **How are you?**, muß man zuerst die Frage beantworten **Fine** und dann der anderen Person danken **thanks / thank you**. Es ist nicht korrekt, nur **Thanks / Thank you** zu antworten.

281 „Das sind meine Freunde" ist für Englischsprechende nicht logisch. Alle Wörter in dem Satz stehen im Plural (Mehrzahl) – außer „Das"! Im Englischen benutzt man ebenfalls den Plural: **They (These / Those) are my friends**.

282 Ein „Deutsch-Englisch"-Fehler – „in der Nähe von" ist **near**.

283 In der direkten Rede ist die Wortstellung in einer Frage: Fragewort – Prädikat (Satzaussage) – Subjekt, z.B. **Who are you?** In der indirekten Rede ist die Wortstellung: Fragewort – Subjekt – Prädikat, z.B. **She asked me who I was**.

284 „Er ist der Mann, der Tennis spielt" ist **He's the man who plays tennis**, nicht **He's the man he plays tennis**.

285 **To fly** ist „fliegen", **the flight** ist „der Flug".

286 „Jemandem Feuer geben" ist **to give somebody a light**.

287 **To exist** wird niemals in der Progressiv-Form (in der …ing-Form) verwendet.

288 „Um sechs Uhr" ist **at six o'clock** – man darf **at** nicht vergessen!

289 „Wie spät ist es?" heißt **What time …?**, nicht **Which time …?**

290 Wenn über einen Zeitabschnitt gesprochen wird, wird **for** verwendet, z.B. **for ten years**. Wenn man über einen Zeitpunkt (den Anfang eines Zeitabschnitts) spricht, muß **since** benutzt werden, z.B. **since 1980**.

291 Wenn man jemandem etwas gibt, sollte man sagen **Here you are** (Bitte, Bitte sehr).

292 Bei 5, 10, 20, 25 wird normalerweise das Wort **minutes** ausgelassen, aber zwischen diesen Zahlen (6, 7, 8, 9, 11, 12 etc.) muß man **minutes** sagen, z.B. **It's five past ten**, aber **It's six minutes past ten**.

293 Wenn „hören" im Sinne von „zuhören" verwendet wird, heißt es **listen to**, z.B. bei Musik. **Hear** bezeichnet das Hören von Geräuschen, die die Ohren erreichen, z.B. der Krach der Autos auf der Straße.

294 Um eine andere Person aufzufordern, etwas nochmal zu wiederholen, heißt es **Sorry?** oder **Pardon?** Die Amerikaner sagen **Pardon me?**

295 **A note** ist eine kurze, geschriebene Bemerkung. **A notice** ist ein öffentlich angeschlagenes Stück Papier, das dazu dient, andere Personen über irgend etwas zu informieren.

296 Wenn man über Etagen spricht, benutzt man normalerweise die Präposition (Verhältniswort) **on**, z.B. **I live on the first floor**.

297 **To change** bedeutet „ändern". Korrekt ist hier **to mix up** oder **to confuse** (verwechseln).

298 „So" in diesem Sinn ist **like this** oder **like that**. Wenn man von sich selber spricht, sagt man **like this**, wenn man von anderen Personen spricht, heißt es **like that**.

299 Ein „Deutsch-Englisch"-Fehler – „heute morgen" ist nicht **today morning**, sondern **this morning**.

300 „Muttergesellschaft" ist **parent company**, „Tochtergesellschaft" ist **subsidiary**.

301 Winter können nicht **strong** sein, sondern **bad** oder **hard**.

302 **Strong** ist „physisch stark". Wenn man von Disziplin spricht, heißt es **strict** (streng).

303 **Concentrate** wird niemals zusammen mit den Reflexivpronomen (rückbezügliche Fürwörter) **myself / yourself / himself** etc. benutzt, z.B. **I can't concentrate**, nicht **I can't concentrate myself**.

304 Wenn man über ein Datum spricht, sollte man die Präposition (Verhältniswort) **on** verwenden. Eine Ausnahme ist der typische Beginn eines Geschäftsbriefs **Thank you for your letter of the second of May**.

305 Zusammen mit dem Verb (Tätigkeitswort) **to be (am, are, is etc.)** muß ein Adjektiv (Eigenschaftswort), nicht ein Adverb (Umstandswort) verwendet werden, z.B. **It's cold**, nicht **It's coldly**.

306 Die korrekte Präposition (Verhältniswort) bei Wochentagen lautet **on**, nicht **at**, z.B. **on Friday, on Sunday**.

307 Viele Deutsche verwechseln **would** „würde(n)" mit **wanted** „wollte(n)".

308 Es gibt zwei Möglichkeiten – man verwendet entweder das Adjektiv (Eigenschaftswort) **good** vor der Sprache, z.B. **He speaks good English**, oder das Adverb (Umstandswort) **well** nach der Sprache, z.B. **He speaks English well**.

309 Ein „Deutsch-Englisch"-Fehler – „Es ist egal" ist nicht **It's equal**, sondern **It doesn't matter**.

310 „Einmal die Woche" oder „einmal in der Woche" ist **once a week**.

311 Wenn man vom Haarschopf einer Person spricht, wird **hair** im Singular verwendet, z.B. **Her hair is beautiful**.

312 In der deutschen Umgangssprache kann man die Frage **Where shall I put your book?** mit „Tu's bitte auf den Tisch" beantworten. Im Englischen muß man sagen **Put it on the table, please**.

313 Die Adjektive (Eigenschaftswörter) **heavy / light** (schwer / leicht), bezeichnen das Gewicht, z.B. **A ninety-kilo man is heavy, a forty-kilo woman is light**. Wenn über Arbeit oder Probleme gesprochen wird, werden **hard / easy** oder **difficult / simple** benutzt.

314 „Eine Erfahrung machen" wird im Englischen mit „haben" übersetzt, z.B. **I had a funny experience in Madrid** (Ich habe in Madrid etwas Komisches erlebt), statt **I made a funny experience in Madrid**.

315 Man darf in einem Satz wie folgt nicht das **as** vergessen, z.B. **Would you please be so kind as to give me that book?**

316 In der Regel benutzt man **the** nicht zusammen mit Straßennamen.

317 Ein „Deutsch-Englisch"-Fehler – „der, die, das eine ..." ist nicht **the one ...**, sondern **one of them ...** oder einfach **one ...**, z.B. **I saw two cars – one (of them) was new, the other old**.

318 **Who** kann als Fragewort (**Who speaks French?**) oder als Relativpronomen (bezügliches Fürwort) eingesetzt werden, z.B. **The man who died was Italian**, aber im folgenden Satz muß man **whoever** sagen, z.B. **Whoever says that is lying!** (Wer das sagt, lügt!). Eine andere (modernere) Möglichkeit ist die Form **Anybody that (who) ...**, z.B. **Anybody that believes that story must be crazy!**

319 Für Reiserouten ist **via** die korrekte Übersetzung von „über", nicht **over** oder **about**.

320 Zählbare Dinge müssen zusammen mit **many**, nicht mit **much** angegeben werden. **Much** wird für Dinge benutzt, die nicht zählbar sind, z.B. **much water, much salt**, aber **many pens, many dresses**.

321 **Warehouse** ist eine „Lagerhalle" und **department store** ist ein „Warenhaus".

322 Bei einer Beschreibung, wie etwas ausgeführt wird, muß **well** benutzt werden, nicht **good**, z.B. **He works well**, nicht **He works good**.

323 Dieser Satz wird leicht falsch übersetzt: „Er verbrachte zwei Stunden damit, den Brief zu schreiben“. Im Englischen darf „damit“ nicht übersetzt werden, und das Gerundium (die ...ing-Form) muß nach dem Verb (Tätigkeitswort) **to spend** stehen, z.B. **He spent two hours writing the letter**.

324 Ein „Deutsch-Englisch“-Fehler – „ein Flugzeug“ ist entweder **a plane** oder **a flight**, niemals **a machine**.

325 Ein „Deutsch-Englisch“-Fehler – **the police** (die Polizei) steht im Englischen immer im Plural (Mehrzahl), deshalb muß das Verb (Tätigkeitswort) auch im Plural stehen, z.B. **The police are friendly**, nicht **The police is friendly**.

326 Bei allgemeinen Äußerungen darf **the** nicht stehen. **Flowers are beautiful** bedeutet **All the flowers in the world are beautiful. The flowers are beautiful** bedeutet vielleicht **The flowers here (in my living room / which John gave me / in this field) are beautiful**.

327 **Do you like ...?** ist „Mögen Sie ...?“ **Would you like ...?** ist „Möchten Sie ...?“

328 **Only** hat nur eine Form – **only**! Es gibt kein **onlier**, und es gibt auch kein **onliest**.

329 **Homework** ist „Hausaufgaben“, **housework** ist „Hausarbeit“.

330 Ein „Deutsch-Englisch“-Fehler – „... die Zeit, wo (als) ...“ ist nicht, **... the time where ...**, sondern **... the time when ...** .

331 In Negativ(Verneinungs-)sätzen wurde früher im Englischen **not so ... as** gesagt, aber die modernere Form ist **not as ... as**. Es ist nicht korrekt zu sagen **so ... as**. Es heißt nicht **Hans is so big as Uwe**, sondern **Hans is as big as Uwe**.

332 Ein „Deutsch-Englisch“-Fehler – „Wie ist Ihr Name?“ ist nicht **How is your name?**, sondern **What is your name?**

333 Obwohl es korrekt ist zu sagen **Who? I?**, klingt das sehr abrupt im Englischen. Man bevorzugt die sanftere Form **me**, z.B. **Who? Me?** Dasselbe macht man mit **he / him, she / her, we / us, they / them**.